T0324449

THE ENDURING VALUE
OF ROGER MURRAY

THE ENDURING VALUE OF ROGER MURRAY

PAUL JOHNSON AND **PAUL D. SONKIN**

⫘ Columbia Business School
Publishing

Columbia University Press
Publishers Since 1893
New York   Chichester, West Sussex
cup.columbia.edu

Library of Congress Cataloging-in-Publication Data
Names: Johnson, Paul (Professor), author. | Sonkin, Paul D., 1968– author.
Title: The enduring value of Roger Murray / Paul Johnson
and Paul D. Sonkin.
Description: New York, NY : Columbia University Press, 2022. |
Series: Heilbrunn center for Graham & Dodd investing series |
Includes index.
Identifiers: LCCN 2021055601 (print) | LCCN 2021055602 (ebook) |
ISBN 9780231192101 (hardback) | ISBN 9780231549653 (ebook)
Subjects: LCSH: Murray, Roger, 1911–1998. | Capitalists and
financiers—Biography. | Investments. | Portfolio management.
Classification: LCC HG172.M87 J64 2022 (print) | LCC HG172.M87 (ebook)
| DDC 332.6092 [B]—dc23/eng/20220111
LC record available at https://lccn.loc.gov/2021055601
LC ebook record available at https://lccn.loc.gov/2021055602

Columbia University Press books are printed on permanent
and durable acid-free paper.
Printed in the United States of America

Cover design: Noah Arlow

THE BOOK IS DEDICATED TO MARIO GABELLI FOR

KEEPING THE VALUE-INVESTING FLAME ALIVE

CONTENTS

CONTENTS

FOREWORD

Mario Gabelli and Leon Cooperman

A TRIBUTE TO ROGER F. MURRAY

When someone asks me, "How do you account for your success?" I give a lot of credit to Columbia Business School and Roger Murray. While I had some great professors teaching finance when I attended college at Fordham in the early 1960s, it wasn't until I had Professor Murray at Columbia in the fall of 1965 that I saw the sun, the moon, and the stars align themselves and knew that was what I wanted to do. (MJG)

When I look back at my career in investing, which spans over fifty years, I feel that the one person who had a profound influence on me was Roger Murray. As our security analysis professor, he showed a great deal of excitement for the subject matter. I still have a letter he sent me in 1977 hanging on my wall. (LC)

We grew up in the same South Bronx neighborhood, which at the time was predominantly populated by Jewish and Italian immigrants. We became great friends in business school and are still close fifty-five years later. We used to commute together (with Art Samberg, a fellow classmate) from the Bronx each day to Columbia. We loved stocks and loved debating investment ideas. And we both agree that Roger Murray had an outsized influence on our professional careers and our lives.

We shared the same stockbroker, Hy Fishman. There was only a single pay phone in the business school at the time and, in between classes, we used to race to see who could get to the phone faster to be able to call Hy to place our stock orders.

Roger taught a whole generation of investors at Columbia between 1958 and 1977, but after he retired, and as the curriculum at business schools, Columbia included, turned away from fundamental stock analysis towards the efficient market theory, there was no one to take over Roger's Security Analysis course. Tragically, the strong tradition of value investing started by Ben Graham in 1927 at Columbia was lost.

A decade later, in the late 1980s, there was a groundswell of support from the two of us and several of Roger's other former students and prominent value investing practitioners such as Chuck Royce and Robert Bruce to reinvigorate the Value Investing program at Columbia.

With Art Samberg, we hosted a reception at the Lotos Club in New York City in 1988 to celebrate the publishing of the fifth edition of Graham and Dodd's Security Analysis, which Murray had edited with Sidney Cottle and Frank E. Block.

We both continued to correspond with Roger over the years because maintaining the relationship was important to each of us. As Roger aged, Mario became concerned that if anything were to happen to him, his teachings would be lost forever. Mario thought that somehow Roger's lessons needed to be captured. He wanted to archive Murray's insights, in part to create a living legend, and, because he felt his teachings were so vital, he wanted to record them for future generations.

In about 1992, the idea was, can we bring Roger to New York and capture his lectures, and in doing so, inspire a new generation of value investors? You don't know where your influence will end, and Roger had an extraordinary influence on both of us.

The result was that Gabelli Asset Management Company (GAMCO) agreed to host the Roger F. Murray Lecture Series at the

Museum of Television and Radio in New York City. Roger gave four 90-minute lectures over consecutive Fridays in January and February 1993. Although Roger was eighty-one at the time, he delivered each lecture without using a single note.

In retrospect, the 1993 lecture series created a spark that was responsible for the resurgence of value investing at Columbia Business School. We invited Meyer Feldberg, the Dean of the business school at the time, to attend these lectures. Feldberg in turn invited a newly tenured professor, Bruce Greenwald, to join him at the event.

Greenwald was so impressed by the lectures that he convinced Roger to return to the classroom. With Roger's commitment, Greenwald launched a new course in the fall of 1993 entitled *The Fundamentals of Investing: Approaches to Value: An Advanced Seminar*, which Greenwald co-taught with Roger. It was the last time Roger was in a Columbia classroom. The course was a huge success, and Greenwald taught the course on his own for the next twenty-four years until Greenwald retired in 2018.

Roger was inducted into the GAMCO Management Hall of Fame on May 18, 1996, and was honored at a black-tie dinner that evening at the American Museum of Natural History in recognition of his contribution to creating wealth for the GAMCO clients. The GAMCO Management Hall of Fame was established in 1990 to honor individuals for their outstanding contributions to enhancing shareholder value.

GAMCO launched the Graham & Dodd, Murray, Greenwald Award for Distinguished Value Investors in 2005. The award is presented yearly at the GAMCO Annual Client Symposium.

The Gabelli School of Business at Fordham and Columbia University Business School joined forces on April 17, 2013, to honor and celebrate value investing and the men and women who have advanced the discipline through the years. The event was titled "Value Investing 20 Years Later: A Celebration of the Roger Murray Lecture Series, 1993–2013." The event was sponsored by Gabelli Asset Management Company and hosted at the Paley Center for Media in Manhattan, the same place Murray gave his original lectures two decades prior. Speakers at the event talked of how Murray's influence carries weight even today in both the private sectors of finance and in academia at Fordham and Columbia.

We both owe a tremendous amount of gratitude to our
     former professor, Roger Murray.
Mario Gabelli (MJG)
Leon Cooperman (LC)
February 2022

A PERSONAL TRIBUTE TO PROFESSOR ROGER MURRAY

James Russell Kelly

S ometimes you get lucky in life. That certainly happened to me when I was accepted into Professor Roger Murray's course in security analysis at Columbia Business School (CBS) in 1968. At that time, Murray was teaching as an adjunct professor, having resigned his endowed chair as the S. Sloan Colt Professor of Banking and Finance in 1965 to join the College Retirement Equities Fund (CREF).

The late 1960s was a period of violent anti–Vietnam War protests in the United States, and Columbia was at the epicenter. In April 1968, Mark Rudd, an erstwhile student and leader of the Columbia branch of Students for a Democratic Society (SDS), led a student insurrection whose participants occupied four buildings on campus and threatened to shut down the entire university.[1]

I distinctly remember walking one morning from the subway station at 116th Street through the gates of Columbia and past Lowe Library to Uris Hall, the home of Columbia Business School. SDS members had invaded Lowe Library and looted the president's office. Students were hanging out of the windows as I walked by on my way to class. These student-led protests were particularly galling for me and several of my fellow business school classmates who had served in the U.S. military in Vietnam prior to enrolling at Columbia. Several days later, the New York City police arrived and forcibly removed all the protesters from the buildings.

This episode was reported in an article in *Forbes* magazine entitled "The Whiz Kids,"[2] which portrayed the courage of the business school students and featured the extraordinary talent of the students in the class of 1969, which included Henry Kravis, cofounder of Kohlberg Kravis Roberts (KKR); Erskine Bowles, chief of staff to President Clinton; J. T. Battenberg, CEO, Delphi Automotive; Lew Frankfort, CEO, Coach; Max Chapman, president, Kidder Peabody; and Peter Cohen, CEO, Shearson Lehman.

I suspect that Professor Murray was equally horrified as were his students about the insurrection, but he was very stoic in his response. He focused on the subject of each lecture and did not engage in any political commentary.

It is challenging for today's reader to imagine the bizarre nature of Professor Murray's teaching environment during this period. It was a time of violent social upheaval. In addition to the Columbia student insurrection, Martin Luther King was assassinated on April 4, 1968; Robert F. Kennedy was assassinated on June 5, 1968; and Richard Nixon was elected president on November 7, 1968.

It also might be difficult to imagine how primitive were the tools for students of security analysis at that time:

- There were no personal computers—only first-generation IBM mainframes, and only for institutional use.
- There was no internet.
- There were no Excel spreadsheets—all financial analysis was done manually on accounting paper.
- There was no word processing—all research reports were typed on a manual typewriter.
- There was no CNBC, Bloomberg, or FactSet—stock transactions were transmitted on a paper ticker tape, which had to be inspected manually, and the only news available was printed on a scrolling Dow Jones news ticker.

- There was no efficient market hypothesis or modern portfolio theory—the only avant-garde financial theory being taught at that time was the Modigliani-Miller theorem, which stated that the capital structure of a corporation is not a factor in its valuation. That theory never made much sense to me as a student, but we had to learn it anyway in corporate finance courses. I am thankful that Roger Murray did not believe it either.

One timeless theory was first taught at Columbia in 1927 by Benjamin Graham and David Dodd, and then carried forward by professors Roger Murray, Bruce Greenwald, and Tano Santos. It is known today as value investing, but it is just fundamental security analysis designed to determine the intrinsic value of a company.

Murray was an extraordinary academic and financial industry leader, as you will soon learn in reading this wonderful book. My personal recollections of him are still vivid. He was 5'10", very thin, and always formally dressed in a vested dark suit, white shirt, and tie, with his Phi Beta Kappa key proudly displayed.

His teaching style was also formal, which was the standard at that time. In contrast to his lecturing style, he was a friendly, welcoming mentor. I met with him several times after class as well as after graduation to seek his advice.

He was also a tough grader. I remember writing my term research report on Radio Corporation of America (RCA), which was the hot technology stock of its era. His comments cut right to the core, citing my lack of focus on identifying the key variable of profitability. I have been much more focused in my analysis ever since that criticism.

A major recurring theme in Murray's lectures was the rapidly growing importance of pensions in society. To a group of youthful students, retirement was not exactly a captivating topic. Little did we know about Murray's prominent role in the development of pension fund investing at CREF or in the passage of legislation that included Keogh plans and individual retirement accounts (IRAs).

Murray taught a full generation of students from 1958 until his retirement in 1977.[3] During this period, he carried the torch of value investing that Ben Graham passed on to him before retiring to California. Many of Murray's students went on to great success as value investors, and the flame of that torch still burns brightly today!

—James Russell Kelly,
Columbia Business School, Class of 1969

PREFACE

The twenty-fifth anniversary of Roger F. Murray's 1993 lecture series at the Museum of Television & Radio (MT&R; now the Paley Center) in New York City triggered the idea for this book. We felt that writing a biography of Roger Murray was important because he served as the bridge between Benjamin Graham and modern-day value investing at Columbia Business School.[1]

The short version of the story begins in 1956, when Professor Murray took over teaching the seminar on security analysis from Benjamin Graham. Graham had started teaching the course in 1927, and Murray taught the course for the next twenty-one years to more than 2,000 MBA students, many of whom went on to be highly successful investors. Unfortunately, there was no one to take over teaching the course when Murray retired in 1977, and it went dormant for sixteen years. Murray came out of retirement in 1993 to give four ninety-minute lectures at the bequest of Mario Gabelli. Professor Bruce Greenwald attended the lectures and convinced Murray to teach one last course at Columbia Business School (CBS) in the fall of 1993. That single course relaunched the value investing program at Columbia.

We also felt that it was important to place Murray in historical context. Graham began teaching security analysis at a time when there were few, if any, professional security analysts (analysts were called statisticians at that time). The first edition of *Security Analysis* was published in 1934, the same year that the U.S. Congress passed the 1934 Security Exchange Act. It was the beginning of the professionalization of security analysis and value investing. Although Graham was a superb teacher, he was also an accomplished professional investor. These combined skills were important to his success in the classroom. By the time Murray began teaching at Columbia Business School in 1956, money management had become institutionalized and professional analysts had become significantly more sophisticated in their discipline. Murray was also a successful professional investor. However, Murray's experience differed from Graham's in that he worked his entire professional career at Bankers Trust, which was a large financial institution during Murray's tenure. Murray was trained as an institutional money manager, and he brought that discipline to the classroom. In fact, it was Murray's emphasis on rigor and discipline that is his most significant contribution to value investing and what had the greatest influence on his students.

We were drawn to this project because we have both been involved with the value investing program at Columbia Business School since the early 1990s. Paul Johnson taught his first course on security analysis in the fall of 1992. As this book went into production, he had just completed his thirtieth year as an adjunct professor and taught his fiftieth semester-long course. During that time, he has taught value investing and security analysis to approximately 3,000 full-time and executive MBA students. Paul Sonkin graduated from Columbia Business School with an MBA in May 1995. He took two courses from Johnson while in the program; after graduating, he was Johnson's teaching assistant in the fall of 1995. Sonkin became an adjunct professor in the fall of 1996 and taught a seminar on fundamental research techniques. He then launched the school's first applied value investing (AVI) course in the fall of 1998. Sonkin taught as an adjunct professor for seventeen years.

Johnson was coauthor, with Professor Emeritus Bruce Green-wald, of the history of value investing at Columbia in *Columbia Business School: A Century of Ideas*, a book celebrating the school's 100-year anniversary, and Sonkin did research on the history of Roger Murray's role in the value investing program at Columbia in 2013 for the twentieth anniversary of Murray's 1993 lectures. Writing the Murray biography was a natural extension of our prior research.

Both Pauls benefited greatly from their relationship with Professor Bruce Greenwald, professionally and as professors in the classroom. The full story is told in the book that follows, but the short version is that Greenwald attended the 1993 Murray lectures at the bequest of dean of the Columbia Business School at the time, Meyer Feldberg. Greenwald was so taken with the elegance and clarity of Murray's lectures that he decided to enlist Murray to coteach a course on value investing in the fall of 1993, which subsequently served as the relaunch of the value investing program at Columbia. Sonkin took Greenwald's course in the fall of 1994. Johnson and Sonkin cotaught the course in the fall of 1997, when Greenwald was on sabbatical. Johnson taught the course again in 2004 during Greenwald's next sabbatical. Sonkin and Greenwald coauthored *Value Investing: From Buffett and Beyond*, which originally was published in 2001. It has been a rich collaboration over the years for both authors.

We teamed up to write *Pitch the Perfect Investment*, which was published in 2017, and are excited to team up again on *The Enduring Value of Roger Murray*. We hope you enjoy learning about Murray's life, his philanthropic endeavors, his passion for and significant contribution to the private pension fund industry, his influence on the evolution of security analysis, his lifelong commitment to teaching, and how his enthusiasm for value investing is alive at Columbia Business School to this day. After completing our work on this biography, we feel that Roger Murray was truly a great man and that his story should be told.

ACKNOWLEDGMENTS

T he *Enduring Value of Roger Murray* is dedicated to Mario Gabelli. Since graduating from Columbia Business School (CBS) in 1967, Gabelli has been one of the strongest supporters of the security analysis program at the school. Without his efforts, the 1993 Murray lectures at the Museum of Television & Radio (MT&R; now the Paley Center) would never had taken place, and it is unlikely that value investing would have returned to Columbia Business School in the form that it did.

We are extremely grateful to Roger F. Murray III, Professor Murray's son. Roger generously allowed us to republish the 1993 MT&R lectures and the interview by Peter J. Tanous. He also read the manuscript and gave us additional insights into his father's life, stories we had not heard before, all of which brought Murray to life.

James Russell Kelly was a former student of Murray and took a keen interest in this project in its early stages, when the authors were dawdling but should have been writing. Kelly published an excellent article on Murray for the Museum of American Finance that was published in 2020. His scholarly research added important details and filled in gaps in Murray's life. Kelly also wrote a thoughtful tribute to Murray for this book.

Doug Jamieson, who has been working with Mario Gabelli since graduating from Columbia Business School in 1981, was prompt in his response to our questions and always had the answers we needed. Jamieson works quietly behind the scenes, but his contribution to everything about Murray was (and continues to be) significant. Jamieson read the manuscript; found numerous, potentially embarrassing errors; and confirmed several important facts.

Peter J. Tanous published an excellent interview with Murray in his book, *Investment Gurus*, in 1998. Tanous gave us a copy of the tape from the interview, which allowed us to hear Murray in his own voice. We have included the text of this interview in part 3.

Meyer Feldberg was dean of the Columbia Business School when Murray gave his lectures in 1993. Dean Feldberg encouraged Bruce Greenwald to attend the Murray lectures and was instrumental in supporting the relaunch of the value investing program at CBS. Dean Feldberg read a draft of the Murray biography and gave us thoughtful feedback.

Leon Cooperman was a classmate with Mario Gabelli at Columbia Business School and a former student of Murray. Cooperman is an extremely successful value investor with a fantastic track record, and he generously read a draft of this biography.

Art Sandberg also was a former student of Murray and a wildly successful investor. Unfortunately, Sandberg passed away in 2020. We had a chance to chat with Sandberg about Murray in 2018, when we launched the book project. He spoke about Murray with great enthusiasm and gave us further details on how Murray conducted class. He mentioned that he had a paper he wrote for class with Murray's written comments but, unfortunately, we were unable to obtain a copy.

Charles (Chuck) Royce also was a former student of Murray and is a highly successful investor. Royce graciously read a draft of the biography and, as did all of Murray's former students we interviewed for this book, had fond memories of his brilliant and beloved professor.

David Samra, James Pan, and Jason Leder were MBA students at Columbia in 1993 and attended the Murray lectures that year.

They were helpful in our understanding of the student's perspective on the 1993 Murray lectures. Their push to get CBS to relaunch a security analysis and value investing program was an important contribution in getting the ball rolling.

Finally, we thank our editor, Myles Thompson, who showed patience when appropriate and encouragement when necessary. This book would not exist without his insight and guidance. We believe strongly that Myles is one of the best in the business at what he does.

THE ENDURING VALUE
OF ROGER MURRAY

Figure 0.1 Roger Murray when he was president of the American Finance Association in 1964.

INTRODUCTION

There was a quiet murmur of anticipation as the speaker rose to address the room. Very few people in the audience had heard the gentleman approaching the podium speak in person and most barely knew who he was, other than by reputation or from the formal invitation to the event.

Although he had been retired for years, he traveled from his home in Wolfeboro, New Hampshire, for the occasion. The trip was not an easy one. He drove for two and half hours to Logan Airport in Boston, took the shuttle to La Guardia Airport in New York, then caught a taxi to the Yale Club, his favorite accommodations in New York City.

The event, held at the Museum of Television & Radio (MT&R) in midtown New York City, was sponsored by Gabelli Asset Management Company (GAMCO) and the speaker was introduced by Mario Gabelli. There was deference in Gabelli's voice when he made the introduction, which was uncharacteristic. The tall, thin, and impeccably dressed man Gabelli introduced was clearly important. On an unseasonably warm Friday in January, the event drew a standing-room-only crowd. In attendance was Meyer Feldberg, Dean of the Columbia Business School, and Bruce Greenwald, a recently hired and up-and-coming finance professor. David Samra, president of the Columbia Student Investment Fund, and two of his fellow students had come down from Columbia's main campus that morning to attend the lectures.

Billed as a series of four lectures on consecutive Fridays, the first was titled "Value Versus Price."[1] In his introduction, Mario Gabelli asked, "And what would you pay for a stock today that does not pay a dividend for the next twenty years, and what was its value?"[2] That was the question Gabelli heard Professor Roger Murray ask on the first day of his course on security analysis in 1966. Gabelli noted in his prepared remarks that Murray had been a highly respected and admired professor for a decade before Gabelli took his class. According to Gabelli, Professor Murray ". . . was best known for his love of the subject matter and the way he conveyed it to a generation of investors."[3] Showing his respect and deep appreciation, Gabelli closed his brief introductory comments with, "Professor Murray has forgotten more about equities than most of us will ever know."[4] And with that the speaker took the stage. Although eighty-one at the time of the 1993 presentation, Murray spoke for 90 minutes without any notes. An impressive feat for a man even half his age.

If modern readers have even heard of Roger Murray, it is most likely because they recognize his name as a coauthor of the fifth edition of Benjamin Graham and David Dodd's famous investment text *Securities Analysis*. Although important, that claim to fame is one of Murray's *least* interesting accomplishments. One could argue that Murray had multiple careers—he was a successful professional investment manager at Bankers Trust, an influential economist, a highly respected professor at Columbia Business School, and a manager of retirement portfolios for the College Retirement Education Fund. As this story will show, Murray was a man of many accomplishments.

We tend to think that we live in the most complex and uncertain times. This trait appears to be human nature and probably represents a lack of appreciation for the uncertainty faced in the past and a blindness toward how current times will look in retrospect in the future. It might be true in Murray's case. Roger Franklin Murray II was born on October 11, 1911, and lived to be eighty-six years old.

Before he was thirty, the country had experienced a world war, a stock market and economic boom, a global pandemic, a stock market crash, the Great Depression, and the beginnings of World War II. Despite these early experiences, Murray led a conventional life, albeit one based on East Coast values and traditional sensibilities. As a point of reference, Murray's family had lived in New York City since the seventeenth century.

Murray was the son of Walter Fletcher Murray (1873–1947) and Mary Campbell van Horne (1883–1960). He had two older sisters, Grace (1906–1992) and Mary (1909–2000). Murray's father had grown up in Plainfield, New Jersey, and was an insurance broker, like Murray's paternal grandfather. Murray's mother had grown up in New York City. She was extremely intelligent, loved mathematics, and enjoyed intellectual games and puzzles of all sorts. Murray adored his parents and felt a life-long pressure to live up to their high standards.

Murray grew up in New York City in a well-to-do, upper middle-class family and had a privileged upbringing.[5] He was raised in a home surrounded by books and in a family that encouraged intellectual curiosity and rewarded cleverness. It was also a family that thrived on self-sufficiency, a trait that was deeply engrained in all the Murray children and would serve Murray well throughout his life. He attended primary school at the highly prestigious Collegiate School, which is the oldest independent school in the United States. The school was located on the Upper West Side of Manhattan, not far from Murray's childhood home at 316 West 95th Street.

In addition to a traditional formal education, Murray's mother insisted that her children learn everything they could about New York City. On weekends, she would shepherd the children to historical and cultural sites throughout the city. By the time he graduated from high school, Murray had been to every museum in Manhattan more than once and probably all other cultural sites of interest as well. Mary also encouraged her children to cultivate new ideas and develop strong opinions, which were evaluated on the strength of their merits and reasoning. The children were expected to hold their own in family debates, and their good ideas were rewarded with verbal accolades. Murray honed his argumentative skills at the family dinner table and learned early how to make a convincing argument for his opinions.[6]

Murray's family were staunch Republicans. They were "steeped in commerce and believed in its values."[7] Murray grew up confident and self-reliant, although with a strong sense of public service, which he demonstrated throughout his life.

The family spent their summers in New Hampshire, which was a common practice at the time among affluent New Yorkers, and these retreats had a lasting impression on Murray. His paternal grandfather John bought property on Lake Wentworth in Wolfeboro, next to Lake Winnipesaukee, in 1896 because of the lake's excellent fishing. Murray's father Walter bought a neighboring property called Oak Bluff. Murray's parents met in Wolfeboro. The Murray family spent every summer enjoying the rustic yet idyllic surroundings. Summers in New Hampshire stretched from Memorial Day to Labor Day. It took close to two days to reach the camp from Murray's home in New York City, but the trip was worth the effort because of the break it offered from the hectic pace of the rapidly expanding city.[8]

Summers included the usual activities like swimming and sailing, and Murray's mother provided an opportunity for her children to learn essential life skills such as gardening, cooking, and even sewing. The children were encouraged to be independent and given a lot of freedom to spend their days as they wanted.[9]

Murray attended Phillips Academy in Andover, Massachusetts, graduating from high school in 1928, where he was referred to as "Rog" by his classmates. He earned a BA degree and graduated with honors from Yale College in 1932, earning a Phi Beta Kappa key upon graduation. Murray's father, Walter, had attended Philips Academy and Yale College as well, also earning a Phi Beta Kappa key. Murray's paternal uncle and older sister also attended Yale.

One of the more interesting stories from Murray's time at Yale was his winning the university's John Addison Porter Prize of $500, which was a substantial sum at the time (a year of tuition at Yale was approximately $1,000 in 1932), for a long essay entitled

"Biography of Thomas Chatterton." The prize was awarded for the best essay on a subject of human interest. Murray was the first undergraduate in twenty-five years to win the prize, an accomplishment he was proud of and spoke fondly of until late in his life. For the curious readers, Thomas Chatterton was an English poet who was born in 1752 and died by suicide at age seventeen. According to Murray, "Chatterton was a forerunner of the Romantic Movement and he influenced Shelley and Wordsworth."[10] Also interesting is that Eugene O'Neill Jr., son of the playwright, was named as the winner of the Jacob Coop Prize in Greek Philosophy, a different prize awarded that year. Both awards were reported in the *New York Times* on January 18, 1932, under the headline "Yale Essay Prize Won by R. F. Murray."[11]

Murray wanted to be a teacher, but because of the disastrous economic conditions in 1932, as he would tell the story many years later, he "had no choice but to go to work and not graduate school."[12] Murray felt strongly that his father already had spent enough money putting his three children through private school and college, and he did not want to be a continued financial burden on the family, particularly considering the severe economic conditions throughout the country caused by the Great Depression.[13]

The year 1932 was not a great time to be looking for a job in the banking industry. Nonetheless, Murray was one of only two graduates from his class at Yale to get a job in banking after graduation. According to Murray, a partner at J.P. Morgan & Co., who was a friend of the family, had promised him a job at J.P. Morgan upon his graduation. Although the offer stood, the friend counseled Murray that J.P. Morgan was undergoing a retrenchment because of the dire economic outlook, and he felt that Murray would get ahead faster at Bankers Trust. A. A. Tilney, then president of Bankers Trust, was Murray's uncle (Tilney was married to Murray's aunt), which made the recommendation a bit awkward; according to Murray, it "was always clearly understood in our family that relatives need not apply"[14] for a job at the bank. Nonetheless, Murray was hired as one of three trainees, instead of the usual thirty, by someone who did not know of the family connection and, as Murray sheepishly recalled, "I was at the bank for 15 years before anyone knew"[15] of the family tie. Murray was paid $25 per week and was told by a senior manager at the bank that he "was being grossly overpaid because they really didn't need [his] services very badly."[16]

The steady income at the bank allowed Murray to marry, and he married Agnes Maie McDede on October 19, 1934, in the Third Presbyterian Church, in Jersey City, New Jersey. The reception was held at the Jersey City Women's Club, and the young couple took their honeymoon in Bermuda. Murray and his wife were married for sixty-four years, until his death in 1998. They had one child, Roger Franklin Murray III. Murray lived most of his adult life in a penthouse on the corner of Riverside Drive and 95th Street. Murray was a creature of habit. He moved only once while living in New York City, across the street from where he grew up on 95th Street, and then only a couple of times in the same building.

Murray's first love was working. His only real leisure activities were playing golf, which he did until he retired, and the Brooklyn Dodgers, for which he was a die-hard fan. Murray would listen to games on the radio and attend games at Ebbets Field in Brooklyn. He was heartbroken when the team moved to Los Angeles in 1957. Murray's son does not think his father ever attended another game or rooted for another major league baseball team after the Dodgers moved.

Murray was generous with the substantial fortune he accumulated over his lengthy career, just as his mother taught him to be. He was extremely grateful for the education he received and spoke often of the teachers at Collegiate and Andover who had made a significant impact on his life. In recognition of his deeply felt appreciation, Murray donated $750,000 to Phillips Academy in 1977 to establish the Roger F. Murray Teaching Foundation. In the note that accompanied the gift, Murray wrote, that he had "nurtured these 50 years a deep sense of gratitude to Phillips Academy for the great teaching and the personal interest of faculty in students like me."[17] When Murray donated $1 million to the Collegiate School in 1982, he wrote, "Teachers, in my observation, either care or they don't;

caring is the critical factor which makes a fine teacher great, an outstanding faculty excellent."[18]

Perhaps indicative of both the intelligence and drive of the Murray family, Murray's older sister Grace also had a fascinating life and a distinguished career. Grace graduated from Vassar with a degree in mathematics and physics, then attended Yale University, where she earned her PhD in mathematics in 1933. Grace then joined the faculty of Vassar as a professor of mathematics and taught for the next six years. Bored with her life, Grace took a leave of absence from teaching at Vassar to study advanced mathematics at New York University. Shortly after the United States formally entered World War II in response to the attack on Pearl Harbor, Grace quit Vassar, divorced her husband Vincent Hopper, and joined the U.S. navy.[19]

Grace enlisted in the Women Accepted for Voluntary Emergency Service (WAVES) unit of the United States Navy Reserve at the age of thirty-six (she had been rejected from enlisting in the navy because of her age) and was sent for WAVES officer training to the Naval Reserve Midshipmen's School at Smith College in Northampton, Massachusetts, where women officer candidates received sixty days of training. Grace graduated first in her class of eight hundred WAVES officer candidates as a lieutenant junior grade in June 1944.[20]

Grace was better known by her married name, Grace Hopper. Hopper was to become one of the first computer scientists in the country and one of the very few women in the field. She became an expert in computer programming and contributed significantly to the burgeoning computer industry.

As her first assignment after graduating from WAVES, Hopper was sent to the navy's Computation Laboratory at Harvard University to assist with the Mark I computer project. Hopper was a natural at computer programming and her shear intelligence, technical expertise, and programming skills soon earned her the spot as the primary Mark I programmer and top deputy to Howard Aikin, the inventor of the Mark I computer.

Hopper wrote the industry's first software compiler in 1952, which was a software program that translated source code into machine language. Hopper helped develop the open-source method of innovation. She sent versions of her compiler to her professional colleagues and acquaintances in the programming world to elicit comments and suggestions for improvement.[21] Hopper also was the first computer scientist to promote the theory of machine-independent programming languages, which she demonstrated by creating the FLOW-MATIC programming language.

Because of her expertise in programming and growing reputation as a brilliant engineer, Hopper was recruited to serve as a technical consultant to the Conference on Data Systems Languages (CODASYL), held in the spring of 1959, which brought together computer experts from industry and government to discuss the future of computers. One of the committees was tasked with designing a new programming language that was closer to English and easier to use than programming in machine language, which was the only way to program computers at the time. The new programming language also needed to run on computers from different manufacturers, a problem that vexed government and businesses alike. The core software in Hopper's FLOW-MATIC language became the blueprint for Common Business-Oriented Language (COBOL), the first cross-platform, standardized business computer programming language. Within ten years, COBOL became the business programming language used most throughout industry and the government. Hopper was thereafter referred to as Grandma COBOL.[22]

Hopper was asked to retire from the navy in late 1966 because she was approaching the mandatory retirement age of sixty. Her retirement became effective on December 31, 1966. Seven months later, Hopper was put on the U.S. Navy Reserve retired list with the rank of commander, and she was recalled to Washington for a special assignment.[23] Her temporary assignment was supposed to last six months; instead, Hopper remained enlisted for the next nineteen years. During her final years in the navy, in her late seventies, she traveled over 200 days a year lecturing to computer scientists at military bases and college campuses. She retired from the navy for the second time in 1986 at the age of seventy-nine as a rear admiral and the navy's oldest serving officer at the time of her retirement.[24] Hopper and Murray's great-grandfather, Alexander Wilson Russell, was an admiral in the U.S. Navy and fought in the Battle of Mobile Bay during the Civil War. Hopper often referred to her admiration for Great-Grandpa Russell as the source of her early reverence for the naval service. Hopper died in 1992 at the age of eighty-five, and she is buried with full military honors in Arlington National Cemetery. The navy destroyer *USS Hopper* was commissioned in her honor in 1996.

Hopper was a great interviewee. She was interviewed by Morley Safer on *60 Minutes* in 1983 at the age of seventy-six. In the four-minute segment, Hopper explained that the computer revolution had just begun and referred to the computers of the day as the equivalent of the Ford Model T. She was correct. Her nephew, Murray's son, remembers that she had a wonderful, albeit dry, sense of humor, always delivered in a deadpan manner. Hopper displayed her quick wit when she appeared on *Late Show with David Letterman* in 1986, where she was a spunky guest, going toe-to-toe with Letterman throughout the ten-minute interview. She even managed to explain to a somewhat baffled Letterman the difference between a nanosecond and a picosecond.

Hopper received more than forty honorary degrees during her lifetime and was awarded the Presidential Medal of Freedom for her "lifelong leadership role in the field of computer science"[25] posthumously by President Obama on November 22, 2016. In 2017, Yale University changed the name of Calhoun College, one of twelve undergraduate residential colleges at the university, to the Grace Murray Hopper College in honor of one its most distinguished graduates. Two excellent biographies have been published on Hopper's life, and she has been an inspiration for many women in science, technology, engineering, and mathematics (STEM). The most prestigious award for young computer scientists bears her name: the annual Grace Murray Hopper Award. Numerous other STEM-related programs have been named in her honor. Indeed, the Murray children were impressive.

Although Murray and Hopper were both extremely focused on whatever activity they embraced and they pursued very different career paths, they were close siblings. When they would get together for the holidays, Murray and Hopper would discuss various companies in the computer industry. Hopper was interested in monitoring the financial performance of the companies for which she was evaluating or using their computer equipment. Despite Hopper's critical role in pioneering computer technologies, Murray never became computer literate. He typed all his reports, analyses, and correspondences on a Remington Rand typewriter.

PART ONE

BIOGRAPHY

1

MURRAY'S FIRST CAREER

Bankers Trust (1932–1955)

Despite the difficult economic times of the 1930s, Murray discovered his passion for investing and found what he described as his "professional calling in investment management"[1] only a few years after joining Bankers Trust as a trainee. His passion for investing stayed with him over his entire and multifaceted career.

While at Bankers Trust, Murray tried to enlist in the U.S. Navy officer training program in 1942 out of a sense of duty and to support the war effort, but he was rejected because of his poor eyesight and for being underweight. Instead, he enlisted in the United States Army Air Forces in 1943 and was accepted to the Officer Candidate School based in Florida.[2] Murray served for several years in the army and was awarded the Legion of Merit during his service. He was discharged with the rank of captain in November 1945.

After concluding his military service, Murray rejoined Bankers Trust and was promoted to vice president, becoming the youngest vice president in the history of the bank. Shortly after his promotion, the bank put him in charge of the credit and security research department.

Murray was promoted to head of Bankers Trust's economic and business research department in 1952 and that year was given responsibility for institutional portfolios managed by the bank. Murray had been an early proponent of equity investing, at a time when trust departments and savings banks mostly invested in bonds.

Savings banks were cautiously beginning to exercise newly conferred authority to invest some of their assets in equities, and Murray advised them to "throw away the yield book—select stocks aggressively and not to worry about short-term timing."[3] Murray was bullish on the economic outlook for the country and felt strongly that the return on stocks over the coming years would far surpass fixed income securities. Murray was concerned that savings banks would be overly cautious in their allocation of capital to stocks and warned the bankers that they would miss out on the strong price appreciation he anticipated if they did not pursue the opportunity aggressively, noting that "timing wasn't everything"[4] when trading stocks. During this period, Murray developed an idea that he hoped would come to fruition—a mutual fund for savings bank depositors. It is hard not to think that Murray would be pleased to see how big that idea has become.

Murray eventually rose to chief economist and head of investment advisory services at Bankers Trust. During his nearly twenty-four-year career at the bank, Murray served in a variety of roles, ranging from investment manager to chief economist, department head to vice president.

Over a ten-year period while working at Bankers Trust during the day and attending classes at night, Murray obtained both an MBA (1938) and PhD (1942) in finance from New York University's Graduate School of Business Administration. Murray's dissertation, entitled "Preferred Stocks of Industrial Companies," was published in 1942.

Murray was also active in corporate governance while working at Bankers Trust. He was appointed a trustee of the New York Savings Bank in 1949 and played a prominent role in arranging the bank's merger with Bank for Savings to form the New York Bank for Savings in 1962–1963. Murray was elected director of the Motor Haulage Company in 1952, a small pump manufacturing company based in New York, his first of many corporate board positions.

2

MURRAY'S SECOND CAREER

Influential Economist (1950–1998)

In addition to his role as a senior executive at Bankers Trust, Murray was a well-respected and influential financial economist and prolific writer. He published twenty-three articles in his career (see the bibliography for a list of his published articles) and, as the chief economist of Bankers Trust, commented regularly on the outlook for the U.S. economy and stock market.

Murray's financial acumen also made him a frequent adviser to members of Congress and business leaders during the 1950s and 1960s, whom he was able to assist with some of the most complex, financially oriented economic issues throughout his career. As an example, Murray opposed a plan put forth in 1952 by Senator Albert Gore Sr. of Tennessee to tax executive stock options, contending that salaries were not enough to lure executives away from established companies. The bill never passed. It is not clear that Murray would have supported the dramatic increase in executive compensation that would emerge several decades later. The egregiously high compensation that some executives have received might have rattled Murray's sense of fairness and interest in transparent corporate governance.

In 1967, Murray moderated a panel discussion for the Society of Actuaries titled "Savings and the Economy."[1] Murray was an executive vice president at TIAA-CREF at the time of the discussion. In his prepared remarks, "The Role of Saving in the Economy," Murray stressed the importance of savings in financing the increase in capital investment needed to fuel economic growth. Murray noted that counterbalancing savings is the desire to consume, which is always a tempting alternative. As a result, the level of savings may be below what is needed to support the economy's growth potential. As Murray observed, "Whether our economy grows at a good rate, therefore, depends in part upon the efficiency with which savings are allocated among the most productive projects."[2] Showing his growing interest in pensions, Murray also stressed that "retirement savings has been the principal sustaining force"[3] in providing the additional capital to fund economic growth.

In 1979, Murray wrote an article titled "A New Role for Options," advocating for institutional investors to better utilize the benefits of covered calls and protective puts in their portfolio allocations. At the time of the article, Murray estimated that only 12 to 15 percent of option activity represented institutional activity despite the explosive growth in option activity, which had grown threefold in four years. Murray felt that professional money managers were missing an opportunity to exploit the benefits of this relatively new financial instrument. Murray would probably be startled at the size of today's institutional options market and the explosion in corporate derivatives.

Murray served as the twenty-third president of the American Finance Association (AFA) in 1964, an academic organization that focuses on the study and promotion of knowledge of financial economics. AFA was formed in 1939 and its main publication, *Journal of Finance*, was first published in 1946. Murray was also a member of a ten-member study group designated by the New York Stock Exchange in 1965 to forecast what the financial community would be like ten years in the future, in 1975.

In 1972, Murray was a founding director of the Investor Responsibility Research Center (IRRC), which was the first independent firm to focus on corporate governance. IRRC provided impartial research on corporate governance as well as proxy-voting services, which included assisting clients in developing proxy-voting guidelines. In 1974, he was appointed to the New York State Council of Economic Advisors by then-governor Nelson Rockefeller.

3

MURRAY'S THIRD CAREER

Beloved and Respected Business School Professor
(1956–1978)

"I had always wanted to be a teacher. I would have become an English professor if I hadn't graduated in 1932."[1] Twenty-four years after graduating from Yale, Murray retired from Bankers Trust to fulfill his dream of becoming a teacher when he began his third career as associate dean and adjunct professor of finance at Columbia University Graduate School of Business in 1956. He spent the next twenty-one years teaching security analysis, business finance, capital markets, and portfolio management to full-time MBA students.

After an eighteen-year career in business, most recently as the chief of economic research for Exxon, Courtney Brown became dean of Columbia Business School in 1954. Brown was a forceful administrator and had ambitious plans for the school,[2] which at the time was considered by many to be nothing more than a trade school. The new dean initiated a redesign of the school's curriculum to improve its overall quality and introduced a required course on the ethical and philosophical aspects of business. After two years in the position, Dean Brown invited Murray to become associate dean and adjunct professor. Murray and Brown had known each other for many years, having worked together during Murray's early years at Bankers Trust. Brown saw in Murray a well-respected economist and professional money manager, with the highest of ethical standards, and someone who could help the dean build the school into a world-class academic institution. Brown was committed to improving the quality of education and academic research at the school, and he knew Murray could help him achieve those goals. At the age of forty-five, after a distinguished career at Bankers Trust, Murray retired from commercial banking. Murray's son is convinced that part of the reason his father retired from the bank is because he got tired of being forced to take vacations. Murray joined Columbia Business School as vice dean, where he managed budgets; faculty recruiting; and, most important to Brown, curriculum design and development.

Murray accepted the position under the condition that he could teach one course. He had wanted to be a teacher his whole professional career and here was his chance. It was not clear that he would be a good teacher, but he wanted to find out. Brown agreed to the condition.

The teaching of security analysis arrived at Columbia in the fall of 1927 when a thirty-three-year-old Benjamin Graham returned to his alma mater to begin teaching a course. It is difficult to appreciate fully the history of the security analysis course at Columbia without background on Graham. He graduated from Columbia College in 1914 as the class salutatorian. A few weeks before graduation, he was offered teaching positions in three different disciplines: philosophy, English, and mathematics. Shortly after graduating, Graham was offered a tuition-based scholarship to attend Columbia University Law School. He was twenty years old.

Needing to help support his siblings and widowed mother, Graham decided to pursue a professional career rather than becoming an academic. Columbia College dean Frederick Keppel introduced Graham to Samuel Newburger, a member of the New York Stock Exchange (NYSE). After a brief set of interviews with the senior partners, Graham began his career a week later at the Wall Street firm Newburger, Hendersen, and Loeb in 1915. He had been hired as a junior bond salesperson. With the intent of learning the business from the bottom up, Graham spent the first four weeks as a runner[3] and then as a clerk.

Shortly after moving into the bond department, Graham started doing research on his own and wrote his analysis of the financial condition of various railroads, the primary issuers of bonds at the time. His report on Missouri Pacific Railroad was given to a partner at J.S. Bache and Company, a competing NYSE firm, who offered Graham a job as a "statistician" (analyst) with a 50 percent increase in pay. Newburger was surprised, and a bit offended, by Graham's desire to change firms so quickly after being hired. Graham made it clear he did not think he would make a good bond salesperson, and to keep him, the Newburger partners agreed to allow Graham to start a statistical department and offered him a pay increase. Although the increase did not match the Bache offer, Graham felt enough loyalty to stay with Newburger, Hendersen, and Loeb.

Most of the liquid investment capital in the late 1910s and early 1920s was limited to bonds, and most investors viewed stocks primarily as vehicles for speculation and the stock market as a close cousin of the casino. Although large industrial companies were beginning to report detailed information on their operations and financial performance, most other companies declined to publish even sales or revenue figures "for competitive reasons."[4] Valuation of assets was frequently a matter of rumor rather than fact, and most stocks traded on insider information (this activity predated the formation of the U.S. Securities and Exchange Commission [SEC]). Few if any of the old Wall Street investors saw any value in studying the dry statistical information becoming widely available, and the analysis often was not a satisfactory alternative to inside information. At the same time, regulatory bodies such as the Interstate Commerce Commission and various state public utility commissions were gathering significant amounts of data on the railroads and on gas and utility companies. Nonetheless, most stock speculators ignored this information.

Graham was well suited to approach stock investing from an analytical perspective. He had developed extensive practical experience analyzing bonds and was predisposed to critical thinking. Graham exploited the general Wall Street practice of ignoring corporate fundamentals by drawing on the growing availability of financial information to unearth attractive investment opportunities. The Newburger partners were reluctant at first to venture into anything as speculative as common stocks, but Graham's investment ideas were compelling and, more important, made money. The partners quickly overcame their early reluctance.

In addition to his other duties at the firm, Graham continued to look for investment opportunities, generally with great success. His earliest recommendations involved arbitrage and hedged positions, with the goal of making money through conservative investments in common stocks, which his analysis demonstrated were cheap. The reputation of stocks was changing, and they were becoming increasingly acceptable investments. The Newburger statistical department changed its name to Investment Research because of Graham's growing success as an investor. Graham continued to advance his standing in the firm and was made a junior partner in 1920, at twenty-six years old.

Graham submitted his first article, "Bargains in Bonds," for publication in 1915 to the *Magazine of Wall Street*, originally published as a popular investment newsletter at the time. He became a frequent contributor to the magazine thereafter. He regularly published articles on bonds and common stocks. Graham was a good writer with an incisive mind and was quickly developing a wide following in the investment community for his insightful analysis.

During this period, Graham began to form the early foundation of his now-famous investment philosophy. In a series of three investment pamphlets published by his firm titled "Lessons for Investors," he argued for the purchase of sound common stocks at reasonable prices. He further stated, "If a common stock is a good investment, it is also an attractive speculation." In anticipation of his later contribution to value investing, Graham began to articulate that, if the market value of a stock "is substantially less than its intrinsic value, it should also have excellent prospects for an advance in price."[5]

Graham had arrived on Wall Street only eight years earlier, but in 1923 he decided to leave Newburger to start his own money management firm. He had the backing of several investors who recognized his growing ability to make money in the market. Graham's initial partnership lasted only two years. Then, on January 1, 1926, he established the Benjamin Graham Joint Account and hired Jerome Newman later that year to work with him. Newman became Graham's partner in 1928, and the two operated together for the next twenty-eight years.

The Benjamin Graham Joint Account performed well for the next several years, as most investors benefited from the buoyant stock market of the late 1920s. Although Graham ran a conservative investment portfolio, it was not immune to the 1929 stock market crash. Because his investments were mostly hedged, or in arbitraged positions, the portfolio held up well in the initial market decline, losing only 20 percent of its value that year—less than what the market averages lost on October 29, 1929, alone. Graham began to cover many of the short positions in the account after the market's initial fall, causing the portfolio to be exposed to its remaining unhedged long positions. Counter to Graham's expectations, the markets continued to decline, decimating the value of his remaining long positions. By 1932, his portfolio had lost 70 percent of its value, albeit better than the 90 percent loss the Dow suffered. These experiences were extremely painful for Graham. The lessons stayed with him for the rest of his career and greatly influenced his investing style.

Graham began thinking about writing a book on security analysis around 1925. He felt that the texts then available were outdated and generally inadequate as investment guides. The most popular investment text at the time, *The Principles of Bond Investing*, was written by Lawrence Chamberlain and George W. Edwards, who dismissed common stock investing as pure speculation. The only book at the time that argued for investing in common stocks was the recently published *Common Stocks as Long-Term Investments*, by Edgar Lawrence Smith. None of the investment books addressed the newly available financial information or explained increasingly complex corporate accounting practices. When he began to take the book idea more seriously in the late 1920s, Graham decided that teaching a college course would allow him to polish his thoughts and help organize his material, an ideal way to build a framework for his insights.

Graham offered to teach a night class in the fall of 1927 in the Extension Division of Columbia College. Columbia's Business School was still young in the 1920s, and most business and finance classes were taught at the New York Institute of Finance at the time because of its proximity to Wall Street and association with the NYSE. Graham felt enormous loyalty to Columbia and wanted to teach his course at his former college. The initial interest in the extension course surprised everyone, with more than 150 individuals requesting to attend.

The course was a success, and interest was even greater the following year when it was offered as part of the college's regular curriculum. The 1928 Columbia class bulletin stated that the Wall Street investment manager would teach "Investment theories subjected to practical market tests. Origin and detection of discrepancies between price and value." The two-hour course, Advanced Security Analysis, was to be taught on Monday evenings in Room 305 of Schermerhorn Hall.

Although the course was offered for the benefit of Columbia's undergraduate and graduate students, enrollment was open to anyone interested in attending. Many of the registrants were working full-time on Wall Street, and they were interested in attending the course because of Graham's growing reputation and investment success. Graham covered investing in bonds and common stocks in class, and interest in the course was at least partially fueled by the strong stock market performance of the late 1920s. It quickly became apparent that Graham was a natural teacher, and he thrived in the classroom.

Graham's offer to teach came with the stipulation that someone took notes during the course. A young finance instructor named David Dodd volunteered to transcribe the lectures. Dodd had received his BS in economics from the University of Pennsylvania in 1920 and his MS in economics from Columbia University the following year. He began teaching at Columbia College in 1922 as an instructor in economics and became an instructor of finance at Columbia Business School in 1925. Dodd was put in charge of the business and economics courses in 1926 and received his PhD from Columbia in 1930. Dodd's dissertation, "Stock Watering: The Judicial Valuation of Property for Stock-Issued Purposes," was published as a 330-page book by Columbia University Press later that year.[6] Dodd was promoted to assistant professor upon completion of his dissertation, and he became an associate dean in 1948.[7]

Although thought of as a duo, Graham and Dodd never shared the classroom as co-instructors. Graham delivered his seminar on security analysis, called "Advanced Security Analysis," once a week, and Dodd taught other finance courses. Graham brought the Wall Street experience, while Dodd was the academic. Graham's course moved to the Columbia Business School in 1951 and became an important course in the school for the next twenty-six years, long after Graham's 1956 retirement. Dodd collaborated with Graham for almost thirty years before retiring from Columbia in 1961.

Graham's lectures provided a structured analysis of then-current investment opportunities. Students would present cases, which were critiqued by Graham and the other students in the course. Graham liked to play tricks with his students. He would ask paired questions, describing the financial performance of two seemingly different companies for the students to analyze. In one example, the first company would have strong financial results, while the other company was in severe financial distress. The students were asked to analyze the two businesses and were surprised that they were the same company, but at different periods in their corporate history. Graham believed this approach showed the students that the same company can appear radically different financially only a few years apart. Graham's message was simple but important: companies change constantly. By simple corollary, a company's stock may be a good buy at a given price at one time and become overvalued at the same price if the fundamentals deteriorated.

Graham focused on analyzing the financial condition of companies with the goal of determining their fundamental value, or intrinsic value. The course provided the first real-world, systematic treatment of financial analysis. Graham coined the terms *security analysis* and *security analyst*. Previously, the few investment analysts in the business were referred to as statisticians. It is important to note that Graham's insight into analyzing companies was developed during a time when corporations were still not required to disclose uniform and consistent financial information.

Although Ben Graham is widely recognized as the father of security analysis and one of the most insightful analysts to contribute to the understanding of the discipline, he had no formal training in economics, finance, or accounting. Instead, he was trained in philosophy, the classics, English, and mathematics. Despite the lack of a formal business education, Graham brought a keen analytical mind and a great intellect to the subject of investing.

Graham and Dodd started to write their seminal book about investing in 1932. Dodd had taken copious notes during Graham's lectures for the previous five years and was responsible for verifying all the analysis that Graham had presented. Dodd also added his own insights about corporate finance and financial accounting to the book. The two authors used the material to write *Security Analysis*, which was published at the end of 1934. Although Graham continued to publish investment commentary throughout this period, *Security Analysis* was the first time Graham presented a comprehensive and detailed approach to analyzing companies and his general theories about investing.

By the time the book was published, the stock market had fallen more than 90 percent from its peak in 1929, and most people had no interest, let alone capital, to invest in common stocks. To most investors, stocks were highly speculative, and bonds were the only acceptable, publicly traded, investment-grade securities. Graham and Dodd acknowledged in the book's introduction that, although investing in stocks had been discredited by the stock market devastation of the early 1930s, a third of American industry was selling for less than its liquidation value. The authors urged investors to look beyond the stock market to the businesses underlying the stock certificates, which was novel at the time and became a cornerstone of Graham's approach to valuing stocks.

Graham's key insight was that stocks often deviate from their fundamental, or intrinsic, value. When shares are purchased below intrinsic value, the resulting margin of safety helps reduce the risk of the investment. Graham demonstrated that investors who consistently followed a strategy based on these principles would experience superior investment results over time.

The publishing of the book's first edition coincided with Congress's passing of the Securities Act of 1933 and the Securities Exchange Act of 1934. The 1933 act required corporations to provide better, more comprehensive, and consistent financial information, with the goal of providing fair and complete disclosure when issuing securities; the 1934 Securities Exchange Act was aimed at improving financial reporting by companies and eliminating stock pools, stock manipulation, and trading on insider information. As a result of these new laws, investors needed a guide to understand the new disclosure rules and the abundance of newly available corporate information. *Security Analysis* fit the bill perfectly and quickly emerged as the most respected investment guide available. As Murray observed fifty years later, "In short, the book is the primer for what we call fundamental analysis."[8] Security analysis was an extraordinarily successful book and is the longest running investment text ever published, selling over 1 million copies in six editions.

Graham retired from teaching in 1956, moved to California, first to Beverly Hills and then La Jolla, while splitting his time in Aix-en-Provence, France. He died in 1976 at the age of eight-two. In his obituary, published September 23, 1976, the *New York Times* wrote, "Benjamin Graham, widely regarded as the founding father of modern securities analysis, died Tuesday. An author and financier, whose investment insights made him a millionaire before he was 35, Mr. Graham influenced a whole generation of security analysts with his pioneering book *Security Analysis*, which he wrote with David L. Dodd."[9]

When Graham decided to retire and move to California, Dean Brown was eager to continue Graham's Advanced Security Analysis course, and he knew that Murray was the logical successor given his strong background and distinguished career in investment management. Murray agreed to the request, but he felt it was important to spend time with Graham before he retired and audited the final classes Graham taught in the spring of 1956.

> I was at Bankers Trust Company managing institutional portfolios. Dean Courtney Brown asked me to come up and give Ben Graham's seminar as an adjunct professor. I said, "Fine. But if I am going to take Ben Graham's seminar next year when he goes to California. I ought to sit in this year." So, I sat in on the last year that Ben did his seminar. That would be the spring of 1956. It was great fun. After every session Ben and I would sit down and we'd talk about what he had been addressing, what he had been trying to do, what he'd been thinking about, and so on. It was a great experience.[10]

Two years later, Murray became a full-time member of the business school faculty as the first S. Sloan Colt Professor of Banking and Finance. Because of his PhD from New York University (NYU) and his extensive list of economic publications, the business school was comfortable appointing Murray as a tenured professor. The new chair was endowed by Bankers Trust and named for the bank's recently retired chair and former president, S. Sloan Colt. Colt was something of a boy wonder. He had joined Bankers Trust as a vice president in 1930 and became the bank's president the following year at the age of only thirty-eight. He was also elected a director and member of the executive committee. Colt held these positions until 1956, when he was elected chair. He retired as the bank's chair the following year but continued as a director and member of the executive and trust committees until 1965.

Murray's first research project as a full-time professor was titled "The Impact of Public and Private Pension System on Savings and Investment," and it spawned his interest in pension plans and drove his initiative to influence federal policy on the issue. Murray also continued to supervise the business school's curriculum revision, which was a critical element of Dean Brown's effort to overhaul the quality of the school's course offerings. Then, when David Dodd retired in 1961, Murray took over teaching Dodd's courses on security analysis, corporate finance, and portfolio management.

Murray took a six-year sabbatical (1964–1970) from his tenured position as full-time professor at Columbia to work as a portfolio manager for the College Retirement Equities Fund (CREF), which at the time was one of the oldest and largest pools of pension capital in the United States. By accepting the new position, Murray was forced to relinquish his academic chair but continued to teach advanced security analysis as an adjunct professor, which was the course he loved teaching the most. Murray returned to Columbia in 1970 as a full-time professor. After more than two decades of teaching, Murray retired from Columbia Business School in mid-1977 and became the S. Sloan Colt Professor Emeritus of Banking and Finance and Distinguished Lecturer.

Murray brought his extensive experience in investment management to the classroom and was a dedicated professor, passionate about teaching, and devoted to his students. Murray loved interacting with students. In his own words, "The name of the course doesn't matter. A teacher's job is to encourage, stimulate and, if necessary, belabor the student to be curious, questioning—to develop his facility in analyzing, interpreting—to see the business organization in operation as a financial officer. Nobody is in a key spot to see what's going on. This is what makes financial analysis the queen of the business disciplines. If you can bring in illustrations to the classroom, the more current the better, it brings these things to life."[11]

Over the course of his teaching career, Murray taught security analysis, business finance, capital markets, and portfolio management to first- and second-year MBA students. He was one of the most popular finance professors at the school. "He was an inspiring teacher who loved to expound on a wealth of subjects, his hands weaving a web of ideas as he spoke."[12] Although only 5'10" and 130 lbs., and always formally dressed, Murray was a lively instructor. When he lectured, he held his hands together almost like he was holding an invisible basketball. He enjoyed fielding tough questions from his students in class and interacting with them in his office after class.[13] He was an avid mentor for many of his students over the years, and other faculty members often attributed students' successes to his guidance and teachings. One of his business school colleagues described Murray "as one of the most intelligent and public-spirited people [I] had ever known, had a wonderful blend of business and educational wisdom."[14]

A true believer in the Graham and Dodd investment methodology, Murray employed *Securities Analysis* as the course's primary text but also brought practical knowledge and real-world experience into the classroom. He taught that securities were chronically mispriced in relation to their intrinsic value and believed that the price fluctuation created investment opportunities for the astute investor. Murray was quick to point out, however, that finding a reasonable estimate for the intrinsic value demanded hard work and warned his students to avoid shortcuts in their analyses. He cautioned his students that precision was impossible in estimating a company's value and felt that investors should give themselves a band of 20 percent above and below as "the range of fair value."[15]

Murray's significant contribution to security analysis was his emphasis on the necessity of conducting rigorous financial analysis by performing historical ratio analysis for any company under review. He stressed that the analyst had to sit down and patiently review all available information on the company and its financial performance, particularly its historical financial results. Murray was adamant, however, that the analysis was useless unless the analyst was satisfied that the numbers were comparable across time. Here are some of the key questions Murray would ask his students:

When did the company change its accounting policy?
When did the tax law change?
When did the accounting principles change?
Are those figures really comparable?

Murray took a personal interest in his students and always seemed to have time to address their questions and concerns. He was meticulous in his review of his students' work and always provided them with critical feedback on their analysis. He went to great lengths to nurture their interest in stocks and the stock market. Murray felt strongly that "the greatest reward for an educator is through the success of his students,"[16] a philosophy that underpinned his teaching style. Even years after a student had graduated and was successful in her or his career on Wall Street, Murray would pen a note to comment on something his former student had written and often would receive a letter or two in return.

In a letter dated April 27, 1992, to Murray (figure 3.1), Mario Gabelli, chair of Gabelli Asset Management Company (GAMCO), a member of the Columbia Business School class of 1967, and one of Murray's most successful students, wrote:

> You taught us invaluable lessons of long-term investing. That the stock market's pricing mechanism is based to a large degree upon faulty and frequently irrational analytical processes. That the price of a security only occasionally coincides with the intrinsic value around which it tends to fluctuate. That, with patience, the long-term investor will be amply rewarded. Lastly, and perhaps most important of all, you taught us to have a deep respect for the facts, to distinguish genuine accomplishment from hopes and expectations, and to reach sound principles of valuation. For that, I shall forever be indebted to you![17]

Gabelli added in 2011, "When I went to college at Fordham I had some great professors teaching finance but it wasn't until I met Roger Murray at Columbia that I saw the sun, the moon, and the stars align themselves and knew that . . . [investment management] was what I wanted to do."[18] When asked later in the interview, "To what do you credit your success?" Gabelli responded, "I do credit a lot to Columbia and Roger Murray."[19]

Leon Cooperman, the former chair and chief executive officer of Goldman's Asset Management and founder of Omega Advisors, was asked in an interview in 2011, "Did anyone or investment class at Columbia School have a particularly significant influence on you?" Cooperman responded, "Yes, there was one person who

One Corporate Center
Rye, NY 10580-1434
Tel. (914) 921-3900
Fax (914) 921-5099

Gabelli Funds, Inc.

April 27, 1992

Dr. Roger R. Murray
S. Sloan Colt Professor Emeritus
   of Banking and Finance
Columbia University
   Graduate School of Business

Dear Professor Murray:

Over six hundred years ago, Chaucer wrote of a well-read traveller in his <u>Canterbury Tales,</u> "Gladly would he learn, and gladly teach". I can think of no more fitting tribute to the man who was unquestionably my most important teacher.

I was delighted to learn of the honor being bestowed upon you by Tulane University. I regret that I could not attend personally, for I very much wanted to extend my warmest personal congratulations to you on this wonderful occasion.

A great deal of credit must also be given to the wisdom of the Trustees of Tulane University in bestowing this honor, for your life's work has been distinguished by many significant contributions to the world of finance.

Your career originated on the practical battlefield of investment survival as a money manager: first, as a vice president of Bankers Trust, and later as executive vice president of Teachers Insurance and Annuity Association and College Retirement Equities Fund. In addition, you ably served as past president of the American Finance Association.

You made a lasting contribution to the lives of every American as the originator of the concept of an Individual Retirement Account ("IRA").

Indeed, what was most fortunate for all of us, you taught countless Columbia Business School students, including myself, from Benjamin Graham and David L. Dodd's seminal work, <u>Security Analysis.</u> With the passage of time, this has migrated from a book title to the generic name for a major financial discipline.

Figure 3.1 The letter from Mario Gabelli to Roger Murray, dated April 27, 1992.

One Corporate Center
Rye, NY 10580-1434
Tel. (914) 921-3900
Fax (914) 921-5099

Gabelli Funds, Inc.

Moreover, twenty-five years later, you collaborated in a Fifth Edition of the book, and updated the time-honored techniques used in applying the principles of fundamental security analysis, an undertaking of tremendous magnitude and an outstanding and lasting contribution to the field.

You taught us invaluable lessons of long-term investing. That the stock market's pricing mechanism is based to a large degree upon faulty and frequently irrational analytical processes. That the price of a security only occasionally coincides with the intrinsic value around which it tends to fluctuate. That, with patience, the long-term investor will be amply rewarded.

Lastly, and perhaps most important of all, you taught us to have a deep respect for the facts, to distinguish genuine accomplishment from hopes and expectations, and to reach sound principles of valuation. For that, I shall forever be indebted to you!

With warmest personal regards, and best wishes and congratulations for an honor richly deserved, I am

Sincerely,

Mario J. Gabelli

MJG/amd

Figure 3.1 *(continued)*

had a profound influence on me. I even have a letter he sent me in 1977 hanging on my wall. His name was Roger Murray, Benjamin Graham's successor as the professor of security analysis at Columbia."[20] Cooperman further added, "As our value investing professor, he showed a great deal of excitement for the subject matter."[21]

For his final paper in Murray's course, Cooperman compared Burlington Industries to JP Stevens. In his analysis, Cooperman produced a ten-year history showing twenty different financial ratios for each company. When he received his graded paper, Cooperman discovered that Murray had detected a transposition of two digits in year five or six for one of the ratios. Cooperman remembers the story more than fifty years later, stating that "Murray detected a simple mistake in a table with 400 entries. The guy was a class act."[22]

Upon Murray's death, Columbia Business School published the following:

> Columbia Business School community mourns the loss of our colleague and friend, Roger F. Murray. An extraordinary scholar, teacher and leader, his talents and enthusiasm for life broadened our minds and hearts. For over 40 years, he was a significant presence at the school, as associate dean, S. Sloan Colt Professor of Banking and Finance, and most recently, professor emeritus and distinguished lecturer. He was a tireless mentor for many students and faculty members who have attributed their successes to his guidance and teachings.[23]

Some of Murray's most recognized former students include Charles Royce (MBA, 1963), chair and CEO of Royce Funds; Leon Cooperman (MBA, 1967), founder, chair, and CEO of Omega Advisors, Inc.; Mario Gabelli (MBA, 1967), chair and CEO of GAMCO Investors; Art Samberg (MBA, 1967), who founded and was CEO of Pequot Capital Management; and Robert Bruce (1970), CEO of Bruce & Co. Shortly after Murray's death, one of

Murray's former students, Kurt G. Hiebaum, wrote a short tribute to his former professor:

> I still feel privileged and honored that I could study under Roger Murray for my Columbia MBA degree. Roger became later my mentor and friend and sponsored a decade of my postgraduate studies at the Q-Group, the Institute for Quantitative Research in Finance, where he was then Co-Chairman.[24]

During the years following Murray's retirement, Columbia Business School lost its focus on security analysis and individual stock selection. Finance academia had shifted its focus from fundamental analysis of individual companies—security analysis—to modern portfolio theory (MPT) and the efficient market hypothesis based on the pioneering research from Harry Markowitz, Eugene Fama, and William Sharpe. Perhaps more important, Wall Street's focus shifted from stock selection based on fundamental analysis to a new era of performance-oriented money managers. The material that Graham, Dodd, and Murray had taught for fifty years was no longer considered relevant.

Tracking the strong economy of the 1960s, the stock market entered an extended bull market in the second half of the decade and *growth* became the investing mantra of the time. A new breed of professional investors emerged on Wall Street. Having grown up after World War II, they had no firsthand knowledge of the stock market mania of the Roaring Twenties, the subsequent stock market crash in 1929, and the Great Depression that followed. For this new breed of young investors, speculation bore no curse. New companies and new technologies were the rage.

New mutual funds were opening almost daily in the late 1960s, and the Dow broke 1,000 for the first time in history. To everyone on Wall Street, these were the go-go years, and the archetype of the era was the performance fund and the new gunslinging fund managers. It seemed at the time that value investing was dead, and its lessons were to be assigned to antiquity. Fund managers were encouraged to trade in and out of stocks in search of performance, which resulted in high portfolio turnover and increased the overall price volatility of many securities. This investment approach was almost anathema to security analysis and value investing. The price gyrations could be almost dizzying at times. However, in a discussion of the importance of savings in capital formation and economic growth, Murray argued that "the exaggeration in price movements caused by this kind of aggressive search for performance also generates opportunities for other investors willing to take a somewhat longer view and capitalize on the opportunities presented by volatile price behavior. My own view is that this [phenomenon] is not going away in a few weeks or months, but the incentives are there for other investors to trade against the short-term, performance-minded fund manager."[25]

4

MURRAY'S FOURTH CAREER

Fund Manager (1965–1970)

Murray left full-time academia in 1965 to join the College Retirement Equities Fund (CREF) as vice president and economist. He was the head of CREF's investment operation and supervised the fund's common stock investment activities. He rose to become executive vice president and later chair. During his tenure at CREF, Murray continued to teach at Columbia as an adjunct professor in the fall and spring semesters.

CREF was established in 1952 by the Teachers Insurance and Annuity Association (TIAA) to provide retirement and insurance benefit plans to the faculties of colleges, universities, and related educational and scientific institutions. The TIAA board created CREF to respond to the rising cost of living caused by inflation after World War II. The TIAA board consulted with many economists—Murray among them—before deciding to go ahead with the plan to create the new organization. CREF was the first of the major pension plans to offer a variable annuity, a concept that had been only recently introduced. A fixed annuity is guaranteed to provide a fixed amount of money to its holder each year, which makes the vehicles popular with retirees. Because the annual payments are fixed at a certain dollar amount, however, the purchasing power of fixed annuities is eroded over time by inflation. A variable annuity, on the other hand, makes annual payments that vary according to the investment performance of the investments held by the fund, typically a combination of bonds, convertible securities, and equities, which traditionally have done a better job of keeping up with inflation.

According to William Greenough, the CEO of TIAA at the time of the launch of CREF, "TIAA turned out to be a natural and, after some early discomfort, a congenial place for the variable annuity to originate. The problem of inflation was bothering some of the executive staff. The invention of CREF was a direct response to the inflation of World War II, rekindled soon after in Korea."[1] Greenough joined TIAA in 1941, when it was a small pension fund, and would serve as CEO from 1957 until his retirement in 1979. TIAA-CREF grew assets under management by more than 100-fold, to $82 billion, under his leadership. Greenough is considered the father of the variable annuity.

Greenough first conceived of the idea of a variable annuity in 1949 and invited Murray, then a vice president at Bankers Trust, to a luncheon to discuss the idea. When recalling his subsequent exchange with Greenough after the lunch, Murray stated, "When you invited me and a couple of others to do lunch to discuss the very general outline of what you had in mind, what you had been thinking about, it was not that you gave us a specific blueprint. Here you were talking about an annuity that didn't have a 'guarantee' or a prescribed rate of anything."[2]

Although intrigued by the idea, Murray was concerned "that it would be extremely difficult to get a bunch of academics to understand, sit down and listen in the first place" to the idea. He felt that "people had been indoctrinated from childhood to the certainty of [a fixed] annuity. You came into this world of annuity income with an expectation that it was going to be precisely the same amount to the penny for your life and for the life of your spouse."[3] Murray had no hesitation, however, in accepting the idea of pensions investing in common stocks. As Greenough recalled, "His expertise on investing in equities was why he was invited to lunch. He had been instrumental in getting a portion of corporate pension funds to try common stock investing at Bankers Trust."[4]

Policyholders contributed premiums to both TIAA and CREF, and could choose what proportion of their contribution was invested in each investment vehicle. TIAA offered traditional fixed annuities, with their predictable annual payout, while CREF offered an annuity with a variable annual return tied to the performance of its stock portfolio, with the associated risk of stock market returns. Most participants elected to put the maximum amount (75 percent) into CREF.[5] Because the CREF product was so new, most of the participants were young and not yet eligible to receive benefits, and thus the fund had large inflows from members' monthly contributions and was not required to make meaningful payouts. As a result, the fund's assets grew very quickly, which made deploying capital a challenge for the fund's portfolio manager.

Murray was drawn to CREF for three reasons. First, he was a strong advocate of education. Second, he was a true believer in the importance of pension funds. Third, he was intrigued with the challenge of managing an investment portfolio with significant, and ever-increasing, capital to deploy. The fund had $450 million under management when Murray took charge in 1965, which was a considerable amount of institutional money to manage at the time. CREF was a balanced fund (invested in both stocks and bonds) with conservative objectives. Murray invested in companies with a long-term view, resulting in the fund's low turnover of roughly 3 percent to 5 percent per year, implying an average holding period of over twenty years. Nonetheless, given the size of the fund, he was still forced to invest $15 to $25 million per year before any additional contributions from participants, which at the time was a significant amount of capital to deploy.

In Murray's words, "I figure in the next 10 years it's going to be a billion and a half dollars. There's an interesting problem. How do you manage a fund of that size effectively?"[6] Murray's prediction proved to be true. Due to continued member inflows and capital appreciation of investments in the fund, assets grew by 35 percent per year from 1957 to 1967. The fund started 1968 with assets of $950 million and collected an additional $190 million in new contributions that year.[7]

As a trained economist, Murray always took an economic outlook into account before making any investment decision. His goal in this analysis was to establish guidelines for the principal sectors of the economy by identifying the dynamics of change and the principal determinants of future growth. He spent time trying to stay abreast of the latest econometric models in use at the time. He liked to incorporate long-range studies coming out of governments, think tanks, and private industry into his analysis and apply his own perspective to them. As Murray commented in 1968, "Investment decisions are oriented to the fundamental approach with an economic appraisal of the market. We have staying power—if the fundamentals are right we can do a job relatively few investors are able to do. If we like the long-term outlook—even if the next year or two doesn't look good—we can stay in the [stock] until it turns up."[8]

One of the challenges Murray faced as a long-term, contrarian investor was trying to determine if a negative change in a company's financial performance was a temporary cyclical one rather than a permanent structural adjustment. Murray was aware of this uncertainty: "There are days you don't know. It could be a structural change and I could be pouring money down a rat hole."[9] While passionate about equity investing and the potential attractive returns, Murray was a cautious investor. Although he could have been more aggressive in his investment style because his fund was part of a much larger organization, he maintained, "We're just not about to play games with people's retirement income. I have seen a lot of stars go by the horizon."[10] Murray further articulated the challenge he faced managing a large institutional portfolio, "We are still groping, still researching and developing some systems of decision-making where we don't rely on the instinct, intuition, or flair that someone has. 225,000 teachers shouldn't be dependent on my flair for their lifetime savings. Most of them hold no other major resource." Furthermore, Murray states " . . . the goals of CREF are sufficiently long range to permit a relatively conservative pace. Total return from the portfolio is what matters."[11]

Murray brought more than just a financial focus to the role of managing other people's retirement savings. He was never reluctant to vote or take a stand against management if he thought one of their proposals would be opposed by his investors. There was significant social unrest at the time and, in anticipation of today's emphasis on environmental, social, and governmental (ESG) investing, his constituents [college professors] were highly vocal on questions of social justice and felt strongly about the types of companies Murray held in their retirement portfolio.[12] Murray took that responsibility seriously.

Murray was elected chair of the CREF finance committee and promoted to executive vice president in 1967, two years after joining the firm. During his tenure at CREF, he was directly involved in managing the equity research department, were he had twelve analysts reporting directly to him. Similar to his hands-on approach to interacting with students as a professor, Murray met with the analysts regularly and took a keen interest in their research. To show his direct involvement in managing the fund, Murray would meet with the research analysts for a couple of hours every two weeks to discuss general business matters and his outlook on the economy and the stock market. Murray also took a personal interest in his fund's holders, "I answer all of the letters personally and it's not burdensome."[13] The CREF board also established two special committees at Murray's recommendation to make an extensive study of methods for managing large-scale equity funds.

Although Murray was busy as manager of the fund, member of the boards of five different financial corporations, trustee of five organizations, and adjunct professor, Murray never seemed pressed for time. He always was able to juggle his commitments without anyone feeling that he was distracted or in a hurry. He had a relaxed manner, was quick to catch a joke, and laughed vigorously to show his appreciation of the humor.[14]

Murray retired from CREF in 1970 but continued serving as trustee until 1972. During his tenure as an investment manager, CREF's assets grew from just under $500 million in 1965 to over $1.5 billion in 1970. He returned to Columbia Business School full-time in the fall of 1970, once again as the S. Sloan Colt Professor of Banking and Finance.

5

MURRAY'S ROLE IN THE FORMATION OF THE PRIVATE PENSION INDUSTRY (1950-1980)

It is fair to say that Roger Murray contributed significantly to retirement income security for millions of Americans. Murray's interest in pensions dates to the early 1950s, when he published his first journal article on pensions in 1952 entitled "Investment Aspects of the Accumulation of Pension Funds."[1] He made a significant and lasting contribution in the early research on the importance of pensions; persuaded pension fund managers to invest in common stocks, advice he followed while managing pension fund assets at CREF; testified before Congress about the importance of pensions, and consulted with the Pension Benefit Guaranty Corporation. In addition, he assisted Representative Eugene Keogh's efforts to pass a retirement plan for self-employed workers (Keogh plan) and got the individual retirement account (IRA) into the Employee Retirement Income Security Act (ERISA) of 1974.

One of the most important events in the history of private pension plans was passage of the Keogh bill (H.R. 10), which became law as the Self-Employed Individuals Tax Retirement Act of 1962, on October 10, 1962. The Keogh Plan, as it is commonly referred to, enabled self-employed individuals to create tax-deferred pension accounts, which extended the tax-deductibility of pension contributions beyond traditional private pension plans owned and funded by corporations. The journey to establish a retirement program for the self-employed was a long, drawn-out congressional battle. The first bill was introduced by Congressmen Eugene Keogh[2] and Daniel Reed, both from New York State, in 1951. Opposition to the bill was focused on its potential impact on tax revenues and worries about it increasing the federal deficit.

Representative Keogh was a senior member of the House Ways and Means Committee, and he recruited Murray to support his efforts in getting the bill passed. In Murray's own words, "I had been Gene Keogh's expert for pension plans."[3] Murray told the story many years later how he came to work with Representative Keogh: Because he [Keogh] was from Brooklyn and was a fairly senior guy on the Ways and Means Committee, he called the chairman of the Bankers Trust Company and said, "I need an expert to support me, against the contention that the Keogh Act will be too expensive, too great a revenue loss." The Bank's chairman said, "I know just the guy you want to recruit. His name is Roger Murray." And for ten years, each year when the bill would come up, one year in the House Ways and Means, the next year in the Senate Finance Committee, Murray would travel to Washington "and give my testimony that the Treasury's estimates of revenue loss were absolutely unreal and outrageous."

When the final bill was enacted in 1962 it "marked the culmination of an eleven-year effort,"[4] primarily driven by Representative Keogh's tireless efforts. And, as Murray observed, "I had worked for 10 years" supporting its passage.

One of Murray's most important research projects as a professor at Columbia Business School was to direct a major study of the effects of public and private pension plans on savings and investment for the National Bureau of Economic Research (NBER). The three-year report was sent to Congress in 1967 and published as a stand-alone report in 1968 entitled the *Economic Aspects of Pensions: A Summary Report*.[5] The 128-page report was the most comprehensive study of pension plans published to that date. The experience forged a lasting impression on Murray and was one of the most significant contributions in his career-long interest in pensions.

When the report was submitted to the U.S. Congress Joint Economic Committee, Geoffrey H. Moore, director of research for NBER, stated in a cover letter addressed to the chair of the committee, the Honorable William Proxmire, "Dr. Murray's work is the capstone in a series of studies upon which he and several members of the National Bureau have been engaged for some years. Fortunately, the completion of this series of studies coincided with the plans of the Joint Economic Committee for the Compendium on Old Age Income Assurance."[6]

While managing retirement portfolios at CREF and dealing directly with individual pension benefits, Murray made an important observation, "One of the great assets of academia is that you can move [jobs], and your retirement benefits will move right with you as long as you're in TIAA CREF because you're holding the policy." The policy is "always yours from day one." Murray then realized that TIAA-CREF was unique, "I looked around the landscape and I said we've got to find an organization" that can provide the same services for individuals that do not work in academia. "We have plans wherever there is an organized company plan or an organized group from a labor union or somebody else. But [the] . . . people in the world who don't have any comparable opportunity are people who have a lifetime of work where their economic asset is their skill, their professional ability, but they do not have a continuity of specifically employment."

To "fill that gap," Murray thought of "having an individual retirement account where" an individual could have a special account with "a financial institution and have a part of his pay, either by his employer's action or by his own action, go into that lifetime savings account." The key would be to have contributions to the account "tax deductible just as it is for everybody else in public or private pension arrangements. And the beauty of this is that it becomes a wonderful asset for financial institutions, and they will promote it because they will have a long-earned depositor."

Adding to his insight, Murray remarked, "Furthermore, here is the ideal place for people to buy stocks" and "make long-term equity [investments] because they will have locked themselves in through this program and the one thing we know about stocks is that they're illiquid. They're a lousy short-term investment. But if you give me 15 or 20 years, I'll give you a superior rate of total return, which is what you need for your retirement savings." The challenge, of course, was that Murray needed a way to convince the government to support the idea.

President Richard Nixon announced his intention to appoint a commission to study the nation's financial structure in the *Economic Report of the President,* which he submitted to Congress on February 19, 1970. The commission's mandate was to "review and study the structure, operation, and regulation of the private financial institutions in the United States, for the purpose of formulating recommendations that would improve the functioning of the private financial system."[7] The commission was named the Hunt Commission after its chair, retired Crown Zellerback chair Reed O. Hunt.

Murray recalled his interaction with the Hunt Commission and involvement in the idea of creating an individual pension plan in an interview in 1996. Congress held a series of hearings on pension reform and "they were kind enough to invite me to come to talk about how the retirement income had gaps in it, and I gave what I thought was excellent testimony." Nonetheless, "[n]obody gave me a time of day" and my testimony "got nowhere." "However, the Hunt Commission was appointed to study our financial institutions and invited me [to speak to them] because of what I'd written and done in the field of pensions." The commission was tasked with producing a report with recommendations that were "expected to address how we cure the maintenance of fiduciary standards for the protection of pension promises." Murray shared with the commission his idea for an individual retirement account, and the commission staff responded by saying, "Your argument is well made" and "this is what we ought to recommend."

The Hunt Commission's primary task was to make "recommendations that would improve the functioning of the private financial system."[8] "But curiously enough, as you get about two-thirds of the way through the" report, there is "a slight departure." The report talks "about the gap and the availability of pension plans of the individual" and "the potential remedy for this is a thing called an individual retirement account." On pages 108 and 109 of the 173-page report, the last two pages of the report's section on recommendations, the commission advocates the creation of an individual retirement account:

> The so-called "Keogh Plans" (HR 10) available to self-employed persons and tax-deferred annuity plans available to public school and certain tax-exempt organizations' employees under Section 403(b) of the Internal Revenue Code have contributed to an extension of pension coverage. Nevertheless, a substantial proportion of the nation's working population does not qualify for a private, tax-deferred, pension plan program. Accordingly, the Commission recommends that eligibility of *personal retirement plans* [emphasis added] under Section 403(b) be broadened to provide all individuals with the same tax deferment opportunities now provided for specific classes of employees. Moreover, the funding methods for such plans should be broadened to include trusts, insurance plans, custodial accounts and special savings accounts.[9]

The commission submitted its report, titled *The Hunt Commission Report*, to President Nixon on December 22, 1972, and it was signed into law by President Gerald Ford on Labor Day in 1974. One of the key results of *The Hunt Commission Report* was the passage of ERISA, which protects the interests of participants and beneficiaries in private-sector employee benefit plans. In addition, ERISA allows an individual "the deductibility of [their] contribution to an IRA." As Murray observed, "[L]o and behold, this retirement tax feature got included." It is interesting that the Hunt Commission referenced Keogh plans in its discussion of individual retirement plans, to which Murray also contributed.

Murray also served as a consultant on pension fund investing to the U.S. Department of Labor and the Pension Benefit Guaranty Corporation (PBGC). Five of the twenty-three financial articles he wrote were on pensions, and he taught extensively on the subject in his security analysis course at Columbia Business School. Murray also helped design the pension plan for Andover Academy while he was a trustee.

In 1983, the Financial Analysts Research Foundation published a short monograph titled "Understanding Corporate Pension Plans." The authors, Edmund A. Mennis and Chester D. Clark, dedicated the report to Murray, stating, "This monograph is dedicated to Roger F. Murray. His years of service, total dedication and significant contribution to the financial analysts' profession is well recognized and appreciated."[10] Murray wrote the preface to Mennis and Clark's monograph.

After two years of planning, the Common Fund was launched in 1971 by a grant from the Ford Foundation as a nonprofit organization. It was chartered with the goal of managing endowment assets for colleges and universities. Murray was a founding trustee of the Common Fund starting in 1969 and board chair from 1977 until 1980. Murray retired from the Common Fund board in 1981. Since its inception, the fund has grown assets under management from $63 million in 1971 to over $25 billion today.[11]

Murray published a paper in 1986 entitled "The Formative Years: A Founder Reflects" to celebrate the twenty-fifth anniversary of the Common Fund. In that report, Murray reflected, "By the late 1960s, the returns from college endowments persistently lagged the growth rate in operating budgets. There was increasing concern throughout higher education regarding the future vitality of private institutions."[12] Murray added, "As a major donor to education, the Ford Foundation was, therefore, impelled to ask whether there could be some recovery in the prospects for higher education stemming from better management of endowment assets."[13] Traditionally, trusts were legally bound to be invested separately (no commingling with other pools of capital), and they followed a simple but rigid spending rule: only interest and dividends were available for operations, no matter the need. "All capital gains were allocated to principal."[14]

The invention of the variable annuity at TIAA-CREF was what started to challenge the traditional views of managing retirement funds and endowments. According to Murray, TIAA-CREF "established concepts such as total return and market value accounting as both legitimate and potentially adaptable to endowment administration."[15] CREF also managed a single portfolio for all its policyholders. At the same time, "the potential of equity securities was receiving a new level of emphasis."[16] Despite the possibility of higher returns from investing endowments in equities, endowment management continued to be constrained by the traditional separation of principal and income.

The Ford Foundation published a seminal report, *The Law and Lore of Endowment Funds*, in 1969. The report presented a powerful case for a new approach to managing endowment funds, the most significant argument being the importance of total return of the portfolio rather than simply annual income. The report ushered in a new era of a greater concentration of holding equities in endowment funds.

Murray discussed in the 1986 anniversary report the legal challenges faced by endowment trustees when managing equity portfolios and commingling assets of beneficiaries in a common pool of investments. He explained that resolving these issues led the way to the founding of the Common Fund, whose name was a nod to the fund's new legal structure. At the bottom of a bear market in 1974, when colleges were withdrawing funds from the Common Fund equity portfolio, Murray wrote a spirited defense for investing in equities in the Common Fund's annual report that same year. "And by happenstance, the best piece I ever wrote and the one that got the widest circulations was a September 1974 article for the annual report of the Common Fund." Colleges and universities were withdrawing their equity participation in the Common Fund and investing the money in the bond market because bond yields were more attractive than what was expected in the equity markets. The investment committee of the Common Fund felt a need to address the situation. The board wanted to issue a statement and asked Murray to write the first draft. Although the country was in a recession and stocks had performed poorly for several years, Murray felt that the market was oversold and was very bullish on the longer-term prospect for stocks. The investment committee thought that Murray was overly aggressive in his outlook and responded to his report accordingly, "We like this, we kind of agree with it, but we think you're taking too strong a position." Murray's position was that this is "the opportunity of a lifetime, to buy equities."

The investment committee wanted Murray to tone down his position. Although he listened patiently to their arguments, he responded, "I'll tell you what? I've got a deal you can't refuse. I write a disclaimer. I'll say this [analysis] is not an expression of the Common Fund. We [will] observe the freedom of thinking and speech common to academia. This is one man's opinion, not necessarily endorsed by the Trustees." Murray's offer was as follows, "If this [analysis] is right, this will be the Common Fund's statement." If the analysis turns out to be wrong, "we can say, 'That's what Murray said.'" The committee agreed to publish Murray's original draft, and he didn't have to modify the conclusion. And, of course, Murray was right: 1974 was the low point in the bear market.

Murray was asked to speak at the Chicago Analysts Society shortly after his report was published. His message to the audience, "You'll never have an opportunity to buy stocks as cheap as they are now." One of Murray's old friends said to Murray after his presentation, "I've heard you say lots of times never say never, but you, you said it." Murray responded, "Yes, I said it and I meant it." There was no question in Murray's mind: the investment opportunities in the stock market were "an absolute steal."

6

THE FIFTH EDITION OF
SECURITIES ANALYSIS (1988)

Roger Murray coauthored the fifth edition of Benjamin Graham and David Dodd's *Security Analysis* with Sidney Cottle and Frank E. Block, which was published on January 1, 1988. According to Murray, *Security Analysis* is "not just a book, it is a line of thought."[1] In the book's preface, the authors state that "the Graham and Dodd approach to security analysis doesn't need any revision. This is not a revision. This is a restatement of the Graham and Dodd principles."[2]

Murray had reviewed the fourth edition of the book for McGraw-Hill, which was published in 1962, and used that edition for the security analysis course he taught at Columbia Business School. Murray had known Sidney Cottle for forty years. Cottle had been a coauthor with Graham and Dodd for the fourth edition and had been selected by McGraw-Hill to be the senior author for the fifth edition. It was logical to have Murray join as a coauthor for the revised edition because he was so familiar with previous editions of the book.

Because it had been so long since the previous edition had been published in 1962, the three authors of the new edition knew they needed to update the financial statement analysis section in the book significantly. Disclosure requirements and accounting principles had changed dramatically during the previous twenty-five years. The goal was to revise the techniques and applications of

Graham and Dodd principles while staying true to the authors' original insights.

According to Murray, "The challenge [in updating the book is] to stick to the proven techniques Graham and Dodd developed while addressing the recent wave of takeovers, tax law changes, and a host of new market theories."[3] When reflecting on the process a decade later, Murray observed, "It's not easy to rewrite the industry bible. There was always this dimension of the unseen critic, you'd ask, 'Would Ben or Dave accept that line of argument?'"[4] David Dodd summed it up well, "It was a new team working on an old skeleton."[5]

The central concept of the Graham and Dodd principles is that an underlying asset has an intrinsic value, and that value is independent of price. Price tends to fluctuate around that value, but price does not represent value. In Murray's words, "the price of a security is like a stopped clock—it will be right twice a day and will be wrong the rest of the time."[6] Murray believed that securities are chronically mispriced in relation to their intrinsic value, and it was the security analyst's job to apply the disciplined, systematic, and analytical approach that Graham and Dodd developed to identifying mispriced securities.[7]

Murray later stated, "The need for a restatement—not revision—of these principles is greater than ever. Those central principles have been right there since 1934 and there isn't anything better out there."[8] Murray felt that the other dimension to successful investing is the hard work required to take those financial statements apart—"that is what I put students through in my class."[9]

Murray "took about 2,000 students through Graham and Dodd"[10] over his twenty-year teaching career. He used the third edition of *Security Analysis*, published in 1951, in his course when he began teaching at Columbia and then began using mimeographs of the fourth edition that he received from Cottle before that book was published in 1962. Murray later recalled,

> I had fun. In that edition, every once in a while, Cottle and Graham would come to an impasse, Cottle wanted to do it this way and Ben

wanted to do it the other way. They were such gracious people that they couldn't ever go into a real argument. So, what they would do is they'd call me up to arbitrate. Of all the miserable assignments! You can't win in that role. But anyway, I survived and remained on good terms with both of them.[11]

Murray did not get a chance to use the fifth edition in his course because he had retired ten years prior to its publication. Nonetheless, timing is everything. The fifth edition of the book was published in early 1988, just a few months after the stock market crash in October 1987. Murray observed, "When everyone is that bearish, that's when you get the opportunities." The authors stated upon the book's publication "that stocks were grossly overvalued." When asked directly about the state of investing, Murray responded, "Do I think value investing will last as a discipline? It will hold in the future just as it held in the first edition of the book in 1934."[12]

Irving Kahn, one of the greatest value investors of all time and a close friend of Graham, wrote in a book review published in the *Financial Analysts Journal* (FAJ):

> The authors retain the fundamental axioms of the original work while addressing current problems. They begin by analyzing the major methods used to decide both what to buy and when to buy and sell. The emphasis is clearly on analyzing individual shares, rather than total market levels and the claims of modern portfolio theory, the efficient market hypothesis and sector analysis are viewed with some skepticism.

Kahn added his final investment advice, "As most of us would rather be richer, we may give attention to something that may augment our capital. *Security Analysis*, costing only about $0.08 per page, is probably the most undervalued buy in the current market."[13]

Murray quipped about the book: "It is not a book about how to make a million dollars in the stock market in your spare time." The fifth edition of *Security Analysis* is a serious investment text. At 635 pages the book covers almost every topic within the domain of an equity analysis.

In Murray's words, the book's basic tenets are:

> To evaluate a stock as if you were considering buying the business.
>
> To view published earnings as only a baby step toward understanding a company's true "normal earnings power," which may be considerably more or less.
>
> To buy a stock only if it can be bought for substantially less than the painstakingly calculated "central value."[14]

Murray observed correctly, "The new version is dryer than it needs to be. Graham and Dodd had peppered their edition with real-life examples. In one case suggesting 'questionable reporting' practices, you could almost hear Graham's voice muttering his disapproval. In the new version, examples are more scarce and less controversial, the voice more distant and more academic."[15]

In response to the efficient market hypothesis, the dominant financial theory at the time, which claimed that stocks were "efficiently priced," Murray retorted, "[M]arkets are wrong most of the time, prices tend to orbit the central value. It is sort of a gravitational force that causes the price and value to coincide every now and then."[16]

David Dodd offered a nice tribute to Murray after the fifth edition was published, "As our successor at Columbia for over 20 years, no other whom you might have chosen could have done a better job than Roger."

7

REBIRTH OF VALUE INVESTING AT COLUMBIA BUSINESS SCHOOL (1993)

There was no one to take over teaching the advanced security analysis course after Roger Murray retired from Columbia in 1977, and the course was offered only sporadically in the curriculum. A decade later, in the late 1980s, there was a groundswell of support from several of Murray's former students and prominent value investing practitioners such as Mario Gabelli, Chuck Royce, and Robert Bruce to reinvigorate the security analysis program at Columbia.

Murray published a short essay, "Graham and Dodd: A Durable Discipline," in the September–October 1984 edition of *Financial Analysts Journal*. In his opening comments, Murray stated, "'Security Analysis' and 'Graham and Dodd approach' have become generic terms in the last 50 years. The first gained currency because it was the title of the book, the second because it has represented a conceptual framework of enduring value to decision-makers." Murray observed further:

> The development and refinement of security analysis over these five decades have been more or less continuous. The Graham and Dodd approach, on the other hand, gains and loses adherents with the passing phases of the securities markets. During the "glory days" of financial markets, the approach is widely relegated to the dustbin of

financial history, except by its faithful and consistent practitioners. Its advocates multiply in the cold, gray dawns that follow these periods of euphoria."[1]

Mario Gabelli and Murray continued to correspond over the years and the relationship was important to both of them. Murray's son remembers his father speaking often of Gabelli over the years.[2] As Murray aged, Gabelli became concerned that if anything were to happen to Murray, his teachings would be lost forever. Gabelli thought that somehow Murray's lessons needed to be captured. He wanted to archive Murray's insights, in part to create a living legend. Because he felt that Murray's teachings were so vital, Gabelli felt compelled to record them for future generations.

As Gabelli stated, "Roger taught a whole generation of investors at Columbia between 1958 and 1977. In about 1992, the idea was, can we bring Roger and capture his lectures, and capture how he inspired investors? You don't know where your influence will end, and Roger had an extraordinary influence on me."[3] That concern led to Gabelli Asset Management Company (GAMCO) hosting the "Roger F. Murray Lecture Series" at the Museum of Television & Radio in New York City over four consecutive Fridays in January and February 1993 (figure 7.1).

The first lecture was given on an unseasonably warm and cloudy day, and it was standing room only. Although Murray was eighty-one at the time, he delivered each ninety-minute lecture without using a single note. The four lectures were titled "Value Versus Price," "Ingredients of Markets and Value," "Equity Pricing and Capitalization Rates," and "Convergence of Price and Value." The lectures are reproduced in part 2 of this volume. Murray's first lecture set the tone for the series. As he observed, "The Graham and Dodd approach seeks to determine value, as distinct from price."[4]

In retrospect, the 1993 lecture series hosted by Gabelli sparked the resurgence of value investing at Columbia Business School. Gabelli, who was on the board of overseers at Columbia Business School, invited Meyer Feldberg, dean of the business school, to

ROGER F. MURRAY
PLEASANT VALLEY ROAD, P. O. BOX 669
WOLFEBORO, NH 03894

June 5, 1993

Mr. Mario J. Gabelli, CFA
Gabelli Asset Management Company
Corporate Center at Rye
Rye, N. Y. 10580-1430

Dear Mario:

Thank you very much for the handsome memento of the lecture series. It looks just great on my mantel.

I have a footnote to the closing remarks in the last day's session relating to corporate governance. Goulds Pumps bought back the poison pill rights in April before the annual meeting. They may have lost the distinction of having the only former director's shareholder resolution offered at any annual meeting. I interpret this decision as their considered judgment that I was about to win.

In case you have missed an issue of the Granite State News, I am happy to enclose a copy. It was an extremely nice event to join Ben Graham and the others among the award recipients. Charley Ellis made the presentation in his usual fine style.

Thanks again for display piece. My grandson was most impressed!

Sincerely,

Roger -

Roger F. Murray

Enc.

(a)

Figure 7.1 (a) Letter from Roger Murray to Mario Gabelli, dated June 5, 1993. (b) News clipping that Murray discusses in his letter.

Established 1859   Wolfeboro, N.H. 03894   Wednesday, June 2, 1993   24 Pages In 2 Sections

Murray honored for work in investment management field

Last week, Dr. Roger F. Murray II of Wolfeboro received one of the highest awards given by the international Association for Investment Management and Research at its annual conference in San Diego. The award was established to honor Nicholas Molodovsky, one of the pioneers in the field of financial analysis, and is "presented periodically to those individuals who have made outstanding contributions of

such significance as to change the direction of the profession and to raise it to higher standards of accomplishment."

Dr. Murray was only the ninth recipient of the Nicholas Molodovsky Award since it was established in 1968. He continues to participate actively in the AIMR's continuing education programs for holders of the Certified Financial Analysts charter.

(b)

Figure 7.1 *(continued)*

attend these lectures. Feldberg invited a newly tenured professor, Bruce Greenwald, to go with him to the event.

Several students from the Columbia Business School also attended the event. The MBA students were keenly interested in value investing and frustrated by the lack of formal courses taught on the subject, despite the school being the birthplace of the discipline. David Samra, James Pan, and Jason Leder attended all the Murray lectures. Samra was the president of the Columbia Business School student-run investment club. Samra, Pan, and Leder had invited several famous value investors to speak at the school, which was a big hit with the other MBA students, and Samra wrote articles on value investing for the school newspaper. The investment club ran an annual stock-picking contest, with the prize money funded by Gabelli. Samra and Pan petitioned Dean Feldberg to revive valuing investing at Columbia. Samra and Leder then had a one-hour meeting with Vice Dean Geoffrey Heal to help him understand the value of the value investing franchise and what Columbia was foregoing by not building an academic program around the legacy. These efforts coincided with other efforts at the school to reintroduce value investing in the business school curriculum. Although the students were unaware of the growing alumni interest in reviving the program, their contributions helped move the effort forward to relaunch the value investing program at Columbia Business School.

During one of the coffee breaks at the first Murray lecture, Samra, Pan, and Leder engaged Gabelli and Greenwald about offering a formal value investing class with great investors as guest lecturers, like the lectures they had organized for their fellow students. The three students gave Greenwald a hard time about the fact that no one was teaching value investing in the school and that the only thing being taught was efficient market theory and the capital asset pricing model (CAPM). The students then proposed to Gabelli that he invite some of his value investor friends to speak in a new value investing course. Gabelli loved the idea. Perhaps not surprising given their passion, all three students went on to have successful careers in investment management, and all three continue to practice value investing to this day.

Greenwald said after attending the lectures, "Like generations of investors who preceded me, I was struck by the compelling logic of Graham's approach. Because of those lectures, in 1993, I dragooned Roger Murray into joining me in offering a revised version of the value course."[5] Greenwald had what he refers to as a brainstorm in the back of a cab after one of the lectures. "I read Ben Graham and became interested in value investing. I then went to a series of lectures that Roger Murray gave, and Mario Gabelli sponsored. On the way back to campus, it occurred to me that Murray was the repository of all this knowledge. He was the last of a rare breed—an outstanding academic and a great lecturer."[6] In a later discussion, Greenwald observed, "As almost always happens when intelligent people are exposed to a systematic value philosophy it was immediately clear to me that there was a lot to be done to improve the finance curriculum at Columbia."[7] Greenwald convinced Murray to team-teach a new course on value investing in the fall of 1993. "It's always a good time to teach a course like this. It's appropriate to the 1970s, the 1980s and the 1990s."[8]

With Murray's commitment secured, Greenwald launched a new course entitled "The Fundamentals of Investing: Approaches to Value: An Advanced Seminar Co-Taught by Bruce Greenwald and Roger Murray." The two professors decided that, because neither of them was a practicing value investor, they should invite successful money managers to speak in the course to offer the students a real-world perspective.

During the first five classes of the twelve-session course, the two professors introduced the students to empirical search strategies, behavioral finance, and the basics of value investing: accounting, balance sheet analysis, and valuing an asset. The final project for the course was to uncover an unloved or undervalued stock.

Greenwald designed the course to teach students practical financial management principles and to supplement the class with presentations by actual practitioners who had stellar investment records. "We wanted to teach students financial management principles that applied to the real world, and we wanted to use real-world practitioners who had demonstrable success over a period of time. We compiled a list of people we wanted to speak. Nobody we asked turned us down."[9]

The course was given for the first time in the fall of 1993. It was limited to seventy-five students but had over 200 applications—and that was before value investing became popular. That first year, students were treated not only to lectures by Murray and Greenwald but also to classes taught by an impressive roster of extraordinarily successful value investors: Warren Buffett, Mario Gabelli, Chuck Royce, Seth Klarman, Michael Price, Robert Bruce, Walter Schloss, and Andy Weiss. Buffett had graduated from Columbia Business School in 1951 and had agreed to come back to the school to lecture in the course.

The course did not rely on academic textbooks to understand how value investors generate market-beating returns. Instead, students listened firsthand to eight of value investing's most celebrated practitioners. The lectures were a good mix of topics. Each speaker had their own approach and their own investment philosophy. As reported at the time in the Columbia Business School magazine *Hermes*:

> Murray stated about the course, "It's hard to see when there will be time when the discipline won't be useful. As long as we have unpredictable capital markets, we'll always need to study something that's fruitful, useful and productive."
>
> Not only did Buffett and Schloss preach about value investing, but they both stressed ethics. Schloss stated, "I started my discussion with ethics because I think it is important. I think every investor should have high ethical standards." Buffett also devoted the first portion of his speech to ethics, telling students that integrity is a quality they should value highly.
>
> Klarman made the point, "There will always be a place for value investors. Most investors either believe in it or they don't. Once you believe it, you're stuck."
>
> One student remarked, "It was a great class. It's one of the great things about Columbia. I enjoy telling my friends at other schools just what they are missing."
>
> Another student commented, "The concepts are easy enough to understand. But there are only a few people who seem to be able to apply the concepts consistently."
>
> And another student commented, "The highlight of the course was seeing Warren Buffett sitting on the edge of the table drinking Coke and making offhanded remarks about investing. It was phenomenal. Sure, I could have read these things in a textbook, but it would not have had the same effect."[10]

At the time of the course launch, Dean Feldberg explained, "The course builds on a long and glorious tradition, beginning with Graham and Dodd. It could only take place at Columbia Business School. Classroom speakers such as Buffett, Royce and Price are making the course a showpiece the world over."[11]

With that first course, value investing was reborn at Columbia and has flourished ever since. "Roger [Murray] was the inspiration for reactivating a program that was started in 1934, [when] two professors at Columbia, Graham and Dodd, put together a book," said Gabelli. "In a world of uncertainty, they were like the Rosetta Stone in unlocking values and securities when there was not that much data.[12]

Nearly two decades later, and barely a year after the dot-com crash, Gabelli hosted a seminar on value investing at the Museum of Television & Radio in New York City on April 4, 2001. A clip from the lecture series given by Murray in 1993 was played to the more than 200 people attending the event.

The legacy of Roger Murray has pollinated the Gabelli School of Business at Fordham University. The Fordham program offers undergraduate students the opportunity to be exposed to the work of Graham, Dodd, Murray, and Greenwald. Gabelli also funded a research center at Fordham called the Gabelli Center for Global Security Analysis.

THE POST COLUMBIA YEARS (1978–1998)

Murray moved to Wolfeboro, New Hampshire, full-time in 1978 on the insistence of his wife, Agnes. She wanted to be closer to her grandchildren, who lived with her son in Wolfeboro. The Murrays purchased a house a few miles from their son's family and two miles from their summer house, which was uninhabitable in the winter. The Murrays continued to spend summers on the shore of Lake Wentworth, although now with their son, his wife, and their three grandchildren, who moved to the lake house once the children's school ended in June. The entire Murray clan stayed at the lake until Labor Day, when the children needed to return to school. As Murray's son noted in a private conversation with the authors, "[M]y mother was a great grandmother."

Although retired, Murray stayed active as a director and trustee with numerous organizations. He also served as a consultant and expert witness on several banking cases. He continued to help manage the investment portfolios for Smith College and Phillips Academy, where he was a trustee for both institutions. He also served one term as a town selectman for Wolfeboro, having been elected to the three-year position when he was eighty-three years old.[13]

Murray died on April 13, 1998, at eighty-six years old, of a sudden heart attack. He was buried in Wolfeboro. The month before Murray died, Wolfeboro named him "Citizen of the Year."[14] The *New York Times* obituary said the following about Murray:

> Roger F. Murray 2d, an economist whose financial acumen made him a frequent advisor to members of Congress and business leaders during the 1950s and '60s died on Monday. As a vice president of the Bankers Trust Company and later a business professor at Columbia University, Mr. Murray helped untangle some of America's most frustrating problems.

Murray had been a trustee at the Collegiate School on the Upper West Side of New York City for close to fifty years. The school published a short remembrance of Murray upon his death:

> The entire Collegiate School community mourns the loss of our Distinguished Alumnus and Life Trustee Dr. Roger F. Murray 2nd ('28) who believed strongly in the importance of pre-college education. Dr. Murray provided leadership and meritorious service to the school for fifty years, serving on its Board of Trustees from 1949 until the present and as President of the Board from 1968–1972. Dr. Murray's long stewardship of Collegiate was marked by both eloquence and warmth. His unwavering commitment to the traditional values of Collegiate School along with his clear view of the future served as guidance over many years to his colleagues on the Board and to Collegiate School. His encouragement of faculty enrichment and development will serve as a living legacy of his devotion to education.[15]

8

RECOGNITION AND AWARDS
(1999 TO THE PRESENT)

Money magazine once called Roger F. Murray one of the "grand old men of value investing"[1] It is an apt recognition. In Murray's own words, "Through the years we've been through every conceivable kind of market. Yet, value investing remains a fruitful, useful and productive discipline."[2]

COLUMBIA BUSINESS SCHOOL

In conjunction with several of Murray's former students, Columbia Business School established several important tributes to honor Murray's contributions. Room 301 in Uris Hall was named the Roger F. Murray Amphitheater in 1992, and the Roger F. Murray Faculty Suite in Warren Hall was named in 1999.

ROGER F. MURRAY FELLOWSHIP IN FINANCE

Columbia Business School established the Roger F. Murray Fellowship in Finance in 1988 with a $100,000 challenge grant from the William Randolph Hearst Foundation. The first fellow was Maria E. Alvarez. Alvarez was the daughter of Mexican immigrants, and her parents expected her to graduate from her Texas high school, marry, and raise a family. But somewhere along the way, Alvarez discovered education. After graduating from Columbia Business School, she pursued a career in international finance at Chase Bank while earning a nationwide reputation for her volunteer work, which resulted in several awards, including the New York City's Mayoral Service Recognition Award in 1992. Alvarez was selected by Crain's New York Business as one of 40 Under 40—she was thirty-five at the time.

The oldest of six children, Alvarez was born in Torreon, Mexico, and moved to El Paso with her parents as a baby. She worked her way through the University of Texas at El Paso and became an assistant vice president for merchandising at a local department store chain. Inspired by a *Newsweek* cover story on Columbia University's admissions director, she applied to Columbia and won a full scholarship to its MBA program. Alvarez earned her MBA degree from Columbia University after being awarded the prestigious Murray Fellowship. A summer job at Chase turned into a career after graduation in 1988. Alvarez's story shows Murray's impact on students continued long after his retirement.

ROGER F. MURRAY ASSOCIATE PROFESSOR OF FINANCE

Columbia established the Roger F. Murray Associate Professor of Finance in 2005 and in that same year awarded the position first to Michael Johannes. Xavier Giroud, the current holder of the position, is also a faculty research fellow at the National Bureau of Economic Research (NBER) and a research affiliate at the Centre for Economic Policy Research (CEPR). Others who have been Roger F. Murray Associate Professors in Finance include Paul Tetlock, Martin Oehmke, and Mauricio Larrain.

Q GROUP ROGER F. MURRAY PRIZE

The Q Group established the Roger F. Murray Prize in 1980. According to the organization's website, "The Roger F. Murray

Prize is conducted annually to recognize excellence and scientific achievement in quantitative financial research. Each year, three prizes ($5,000, $3,000, and $2,000) are awarded to individuals who present outstanding research at the Q Group's seminars. Criteria for the award include originality and novelty of ideas and concepts, usefulness and timeliness of the results to the investment community, and comprehensibility of verbal and written presentations."[3]

Murray was involved in the founding of the Institute for Quantitative Research in Finance (the Q Group) in 1966 and remained active in the group for more than twenty-five years. The institute's original twenty-nine member firms joined together to explore the application of Harry Markowitz's modern portfolio theory (MPT) to the investment process.

NICHOLAS MOLODOVSKY AWARD

Murray received the prestigious Nicholas Molodovsky Award from the CFA Institute in 1993, an award that "is presented periodically to individuals who have made outstanding contributions that change the direction of the profession and raise it to higher standards of accomplishment."[4] The award was established in 1968 to honor Nicholas Molodovsky, one of the profession's outstanding scholars and the award's first recipient. Murray was only the ninth recipient for the award, established in 1968. It had also been given to Benjamin Graham in 1975.

GABELLI ASSET MANAGEMENT COMPANY (GAMCO)

Murray was inducted into the GAMCO Hall of Fame on May 18, 1996 (figure 8.1) and was honored at a black-tie dinner that evening at the American Museum of Natural History in recognition of his "contribution to creating wealth for the GAMCO clients."[5] Mario Gabelli established the GAMCO Hall of Fame in 1990 to

Figure 8.1 Mario Gabelli and Roger Murray when Murray was inducted into the Gabelli Asset Management Company (GAMCO) Hall of Fame in 1996.

honor individuals (primarily CEOs of portfolio companies) for their outstanding contributions to enhancing shareholder value.

Gabelli and GAMCO launched the Graham & Dodd, Murray, Greenwald Prize for Value Investing in 2005. The award is presented yearly at the GAMCO annual Investor Client Symposium. As described on GAMCO's website:

> The value approach to investing pioneered by Professors Benjamin Graham and David Dodd and further developed by Professors Roger Murray and Bruce Greenwald of the Columbia University Graduate School of Business has been, by a wide margin, the most consistently successful approach to investing. This success has been validated by a number of academic/statistical studies, by the performance of value-oriented money management institutions, and by the records of individual, value-oriented investment managers. Our belief is that the dissemination, extension, and refinement of the value approach

are broadly beneficial to investors at large. In 2005, GAMCO Asset Management Inc., in cooperation with the Columbia University Graduate School of Business, established an annual prize for Value Investing.

The prize is intended to honor individual contributions in at least one of five areas, which serve the goals of refining, extending, and disseminating the practice of Value Investing:

Innovative work in valuing securities in the Graham and Dodd tradition for either particular industries or asset classes

This work may be either theoretical/academic or applied/practical. However, it will extend existing conventional wisdom on valuation in ways that can be usefully applied in practice

Innovative academic research of either a theoretical or statistical nature that illuminates and extends the principles of Value Investing

Work in community building and/or information dissemination that contributes to the widespread practice of Graham and Dodd principles

Outstanding contributions to Value Investing education by students, faculty (adjunct and full time), and practitioners

Contributions to the implementation of sound Value Investing practices within companies either through investor activism or public advocacy

Past winners of the Graham & Dodd, Murray, Greenwald Award for Distinguished Value Investors are:

2005—Joel M. Greenblatt—CIO, Gotham Asset Management

2006—Martin J. Whitman—CIO, Third Avenue Management

2007—Robert W. Bruce—Bruce & Co. (former CIO of Fireman's Fund)

2008—Jean-Marie Eveillard—CIO, First Eagle Funds

2009—Richard H. Thaler—Professor, University of Chicago, 2017 Nobel Memorial Prize in Economic Sciences

2010—Charles M. Royce—CIO, Royce Funds

2011—Erin Bellissimo—executive director of the Heilbrunn Center for Graham & Dodd Investing

2012—William von Mueffling—CIO, Cantillon Capital Management

2013—Michael F. Price—former CIO Heine Securities

2014—Ravi Jagannathan—professor, Kellogg School, Northwestern University/ William E. Simon—Wesray Capital Corporation

2015—Leon G. Cooperman—Omega Advisors

2016—Howard S. Marks—Oaktree Capital Management

2017—Thomas A. Russo—Gardner Russo & Gardner

2018—Christopher C. Stavrou—Stavrou Partners

2019—Bruce Greenwald—Robert Heilbrunn Professor Emeritus of Finance and Asset Management, Columbia Business School

2020—Lewis A. Sanders—AllianceBernstein

The Gabelli School of Business at Fordham University and Columbia University Business School joined forces on April 17, 2013, to honor and celebrate value investing and the men and women who have advanced it through the years. The event was titled "Value Investing 20 Years Later: A Celebration of the Roger Murray Lecture Series, 1993–2013." The event was sponsored by GAMCO and took place, as did the original Murray lectures two decades ago, at the Paley Center for Media (previously known as the Museum of Television & Radio) in New York City.

Mario Gabelli, GAMCO's founder, received his BA from Fordham in 1965 and his MBA at Columbia Business School in 1967; thus, he has strong ties to both schools. Speakers at the event talked of how Murray's influence carries weight even today in both the private sector of finance and in academia at Fordham and Columbia.

Tano Santos, the David L. and Elsie M. Dodd Professor of Finance at Columbia Business School, delivered the keynote speech. Santos was joined by Joseph M. McShane, S. J., president of Fordham University; Donna Rapaccioli, PhD, dean of the Gabelli School of Business and dean of the faculty of business; and James Russell Kelly, lecturer in finance and director of the Gabelli Center for Global Investment Analysis at Fordham. Paul D. Sonkin, a portfolio manager at GAMCO at the time, gave a presentation entitled "Celebrating Roger Murray's Life."

Santos mapped out the three principles of value investing and offered statistical data to back up the underpinnings of the claims:

> Securities prices fluctuate, and sometimes they deviate from the fundamental value of the company.
>
> These securities have values you can actually assess if you have a reasonable amount of knowledge about the companies.
>
> As Roger Murray so beautifully put it in one of his lectures, market prices tend to gravitate towards "intrinsic value."[6]

Santos added, "Should you uncover a good investment opportunity, like a particular security whose fundamental value is above the market price, you know that eventually, if you're patient enough, you will get your reward in the form of higher returns with a convergence of the market price to the fundamental value."[7]

Santos went on to say, "The key to understanding value investing is patience and the courage of your convictions in the securities you have invested in—which is why more people don't embrace it. It can be a lonely road, as it's psychologically uncomfortable, for example, to resist the temptation to jump onto the latest tech stock and instead put your money into a small utility company in Ohio."[8] Santos also stressed that discipline and continuous questioning are also paramount. "The right question when trading is always, 'Why is someone selling what I'm buying?'"[9] He then asked, "This is the fundamental problem with trade. It's a problem with a long tradition in economics. How come, when I buy from Mario, he's selling it to me? What does he know that I don't? That's the key that you have ask yourself all the time when trading."[10]

Like Gabelli, James Kelly took Murray's class at Columbia, and he recalled that he was a tough grader, just like Benjamin Graham, who gave an A+ to only one student—Warren Buffett. Kelly, the director of the Gabelli Center for Global Security Analysis at Fordham, was introduced to the audience of twenty-one students who had just completed the new value investing secondary concentration and forty other students who were currently studying value investing at Fordham. He predicted that the lessons of Bruce Greenwald, who had guest-lectured four times in Kelly's Introduction to Value Investing course, would resonate with them as strongly as Murray's lessons did with him. Kelly added, "Murray had a profound impact on my academic and professional development, and I can only strive to live up to his legacy at Fordham today."[11]

9

THE "NEW" ROGER MURRAY
LECTURE SERIES (2000)

The first lecture in the Annual Roger F. Murray Lecture Series at Columbia Business School (CBS) was held on August 26, 2020. The lecture series was launched in Murray's honor, with the objective of creating an opportunity for members of the Columbia Business School community to meet once a year to discuss the state of investing and financial markets with academics from the school and industry practitioners.

In his introduction to the event, Columbia Business School dean Costis Maglaras gave a brief background on Murray's legacy at the school before introducing the featured speaker, Bruce Greenwald, the Robert Heilbrunn Professor Emeritus of Asset Management and Finance. Dean Maglaras pointed out that it is only appropriate for the first speaker in the series to be Professor Greenwald because it was Greenwald and Murray who reestablished value investing at the school in 1993. Greenwald went on to teach value investing to Columbia MBAs for the next twenty-five years. Also appropriate is that Tano Santos, the David L. and Elsie M. Dodd Professor of Finance, interviewed Professor Greenwald for seventy-five minutes before opening the discussion to questions from the online audience of 500 people. Professor Santos succeeded Greenwald in running the value investing program and teaching the value investing course at CBS. As expected, Professor Greenwald provided a spirited and lively discussion on the key aspects of value investing and, in his typical reserved manner, pointed to several critical issues facing the discipline.

OUTLOOK FOR VALUE INVESTING

Although optimistic about the prospects of value investing, Greenwald stressed that, because of the rapid increase in the number of value investors, the prospects of delivering superior investment performance based on the discipline has gotten significantly more challenging. Greenwald often points out that, to deliver superior results, the investor needs to be on the right side of the trade. To do that, the investor must have better information or a better sense of value than her or his trading partner. Greenwald has emphasized in recent years the importance of specialization as the only way to ensure that investors are the better-informed party in the trade.

Greenwald reminded listeners that value investing is a process and one that has evolved over time. He stressed the importance of being flexible but not to forget the three pillars of value investing that were first articulated by Benjamin Graham and taught by Murray. First, the investor must have an edge, which can be found only by looking in the right place for value. Second, the investor must know the value of what she or he is buying, which can be obtained only with superior information or more insightful analysis. And third, the investor needs to have the patience and discipline to wait for a decent margin of safety before committing capital.

Greenwald was confident that the value-investing discipline would continue to adapt in the future, in practice, and at the business school, as it has many times over the years since first being introduced by Benjamin Graham and David Dodd eighty-five years ago. The two key issues Greenwald felt that need to be addressed more fully is valuing growth and managing portfolio-level risk in an all-equity portfolio.

GROWTH

Before discussing the challenges of valuing growth in his prepared remarks, Greenwald noted that the nature of industry structure, competition, and return on capital has changed dramatically in the past seventy years. Whereas most manufacturing companies in the post–World War II era faced the prospect of diminishing returns on capital as they grew, service-oriented companies in the past thirty years have delivered increasing returns as they have grown because of the scale benefits inherent to these business models. Valuing growth for postwar companies was not that critical because its value tended to decline over time. Not so for the more recent service-oriented companies, where the value of growth *increases* over time. Although these forces have resulted in highly profitable companies, valuing growth has become more important and much more difficult for investors.

Greenwald raised several critical challenges in valuing growth, the most important of which is that not all growth is created equal. Greenwald helped pioneer the use of competitive advantage as a key component of the value investors' tool kit and stressed in his talk the importance of understanding where the industry barriers to entry lie and how well the company's franchise is protected from competitors. Greenwald taught that there are four metrics to confirm that a franchise exists. First, there must be above average returns on capital, as measured by return on invested capital. Second, there must be market share stability over time between the leading companies in the industry. Third, there must be evidence of failed entry by wannabe competitors. And fourth, market shares must be concentrated among the leading firms in the industry. Greenwald also stressed that many franchises are based inherently on intangibles, such as sales, marketing, and research and development, which are expenses that in most cases are run through the income statement rather than capitalized on the balance sheet. From an accounting perspective, these expenses understate the company's profitability and at the same time understate the company's invested capital, both of which are potentially misleading in regard to the company's *actual* return on capital.

Greenwald stressed further that it is critical to distinguish between companies that can grow their franchise from those that cannot. Because it is only those companies that have a franchise that will generate value from growth, those companies can only grow as fast as their industry over time. Greenwald also emphasized the importance of local geographic franchises because they have the most durable competitive advantages, and he pointed out that many of the most successful companies, such as Deere and Walmart, have implemented a strategy along those lines. In the end, Greenwald reminded the listeners that franchises do not last forever and to be on a constant lookout for evidence that a franchise is eroding.

When discussing big tech, Greenwald was quick to point out that not all technology franchises are equally strong and emphasized that most of the most successful tech companies make the bulk of their profits from a focused strategy, for example, Google in search, Facebook in social media, and Microsoft in enterprise software. Because of network effects, these markets usually result in a winner-take-most market structure with extremely high returns on capital for the dominant firm.

Before moving on from the discussion of growth, Greenwald stressed that there is a big difference between a company's growth rate and an investor's financial return, with the latter being dampened by the premium to current value that the investor pays for the investment.

RISK

Greenwald mentioned that there are three basic tenets of risk management for the value investor. First, do not overpay for the investment. Second, do not put yourself in a position to be forced to sell, which means do not use leverage in your portfolio. And third, size investment positions according to the level of confidence you have in the investment's prospective return. Although Graham and Dodd established the use of a margin of safety as the primary risk management tool for individual equity positions, they never developed a way to manage the risk of holding equities at the portfolio level other than position sizing and diversification, which are interrelated concepts. Greenwald stated that nothing exists to manage the risk of holding equities in general, other than hedging, which can be costly and is often a significant drag on investment performance without providing much of a safeguard, especially in bull markets, when risk mitigation is most important. Greenwald closed his discussion by stressing that he believed portfolio-level risk management was one of the challenges value investors still needed to resolve.

THE SECOND ANNUAL ROGER MURRAY
LECTURE SERIES

The Heilbrunn Center hosted the second annual Roger Murray lecture series event on August 26, 2021, featuring a conversation with Tano Santos, David L. and Elsie M. Dodd Professor of Finance and Faculty Director of the Heilbrunn Center for Graham & Dodd Investing, and Richard Thaler, Charles R. Walgreen Distinguished Service Professor of Behavioral Science and Economics at the University of Chicago Booth School of Business and 2017 recipient of the Nobel Memorial Prize in Economic Sciences.

Kent Daniel, Senior Vice Dean and Jean-Marie Eveillard, First Eagle Investment Management Professor of Business, introduced professor Thaler. Interestingly, Daniel, Santos, and Thaler all were colleagues together at the University of Chicago 25 years earlier.

Thaler is one of the founders of the field of behavioral economics, for which he received his Nobel Prize. He, along with Daniel Kahneman and Amos Tversky, pioneered the realization that individuals do not act rationally, or at least in the way classical economics models rational behavior. Thaler not only demonstrated that individuals make bad decisions but showed *how* they make bad decisions. He had a great eye for spotting the faults and foibles in individuals' economic decision-making, which he detailed in his column *Anomalies*, published regularly in the *Journal of Economic Perspectives*. As with many breakthroughs, the initial reaction to Professor Thaler's research among economists was negative, if not openly hostile. Nonetheless, Thaler pursued his research and, today, with much credit to Thaler's tireless efforts, behavioral economics is a deep and widely accepted economic discipline.

The focus of the discussion during the event was on Thaler's book *Nudge*, which he co-authored with Cass Sunstein. While originally published in April of 2008, the book's second edition, which Thaler affectionately subtitled as the "Final Edition," was published shortly before the lecture.

In the book, Thaler describes "Choice Architecture" as the systematic study of how choices are structured and presented. Interestingly, Thaler invented the phrase, and it has become a well-accepted phrase and is an emerging sub-discipline of behavioral economics. Choice Architecture is based on two important premises. The first premise comes from Kahneman and Tversky's pioneering work on prospect theory, which was the first research to show that individuals have systematic biases resulting in predictable errors in decision-making. The second premise is based on Thaler's research that showed individuals have limited self-control. Thaler realized that if individuals make systematic errors and have limited self-control then they will have difficulty correcting their decision-making mistakes.

In their book, Thaler and Sunstein argue that there are aids, which the authors refer to as "nudges" and hence the name of the book, that improve individual decision-making. These aids can be implanted by the decision maker or by another person. A simple example is an alarm clock. As we all know, an individual uses an alarm clock to nudge themselves out of bed. Thaler's research explored ways to structure situations to improve the outcome of individual decisions using nudges. For instance, a research study found that automatically enrolling employees into a voluntary pension program increased participation to 90 percent versus a 50 percent participation rate when employees had to opt in.

In addition to being a Nobel-recognized economist and a best-selling author, Thaler is also a successful professional investor through his firm Fuller & Thaler Asset Management, which he started in 1993 and as of 2021 had over $11 billion under management. The firm's investment approach is "behavioral investing," in which they attempt to anticipate bias-based mistakes that other investors will make without making those same mistakes themselves.

The greatest contribution from behavioral economics, and its close cousin behavioral finance, is the well-documented evidence that individuals do not consistently act rationally when faced with economic or financial decisions. Investing, which was Murray's deep passion, is an area where these biases can have significant negative financial consequences. The question remains, however, of how these individual biases aggregate across hundreds if not thousands of investors. Because, despite Thaler's success as a professional investor, if the individual biases are uncorrelated, they will effectively cancel each other out. The net results would not lead to mispricings in the market and behavioral investing would not consistently outperform.

Thaler's first paper exploring irrationality in an individual's decision-making, "An Economic Theory of Self-Control," was published in 1981, four years after Murray retired. And Thaler's first finance paper, "Does the Stock Market Overreact?," was published in 1985. Although much of the seminal research in behavioral finance was published after Roger Murray retired, he would have recognized many of the individual biases that were later cataloged by Thaler and his colleagues.

Unfortunately, Murray and Thaler were never able to sit together to discuss investing theories, although, interestingly, their paths crossed once when they were both expert witnesses, albeit on opposite sides, in the long and contentious 1986 estate battle over the Johnson & Johnson fortune.

In Thaler's view, individuals are prone to mistakes when making financial decisions. And in Murray's view, the primary mitigant for these mistakes was maintaining a rigorous and disciplined investment process. One could argue that discipline is Murray's most significant contribution to value investing.

PART TWO

MUSEUM OF TELEVISION
AND RADIO LECTURES

Professor Murray gave four ninety-minute lectures at the Museum of Television and Radio (now the Paley Center) in New York City over four consecutive Fridays in January and February 1993 (figure part 2 int.1). The event, titled "Roger F. Murray Lecture Series," was hosted by Gabelli Asset Management Company (GAMCO). Part 2 includes lightly edited transcripts of the lectures.

One Corporate Center
Rye, NY 10580-1433
Tel. (914) 921-5000
Fax (914) 921-5060

GAMCO Investors, Inc.
Gabelli Asset Management Company

December 2, 1992

Professor Roger F. Murray
P.O. Box 669
Pleasant Valley Road
Wolfeboro, NH 03894

Dear Roger:

We at Gabelli Asset Management Company are privileged to be the sponsor of the upcoming Roger Murray Lecture Series on topics of security analysis.

The enclosed memorandum was circulated to our staff and details the specifics. The only open item revolves around yourself and our firm.

I believe we both agreed the tapes belong to you. I believe we also agreed that we have the right to duplicate them for our clients and other interested parties at our cost. If, for any reason, we ever charge a fee for these tapes, the cash will either cover costs or require a contribution to Columbia Business School or your favorite non-profit organization.

With best wishes, I am

We are all expting expected

Sincerely,

Mario J. Gabelli

MJG/kk
enc.

Figure 10.0 Letter, dated December 2, 1992, from Mario Gabelli to Roger Murray regarding the Murray lecture series at the Museum of Television & Radio (now the Paley Center), in New York City, scheduled for January to February 1993.

10

LECTURE 1—VALUE VERSUS PRICE

(January 22, 1993)

MARIO J. GABELLI: And what would you pay for a stock that does not pay a dividend twenty years from now, and what was its value? That was the first question I heard when I walked into Roger Murray's course of security analysis in 1966 at Columbia Business School. Professor Murray was at Columbia for ten years prior to that and was best known for the students and the love of the subject matter and the way he conveyed that subject matter to a generation of investors. And he continues to do that today.

We are particularly privileged to have this individual who knows more about equities than most of us . . . and has forgotten more about equities than most of us will ever learn. Roger is going to talk for an hour and a half, uninterrupted, for the next four weeks on various aspects of valuation. Today's lecture will be on value versus price. Next week's will be the ingredients of the market and value, and without my going into the other subject matters, the tapes will be available. And, Professor Murray, it is all yours—the classroom is yours.

ROGER F. MURRAY: Thank you, Mario, and welcome to all of you. What I am going to try and do in this series is to take a look at some of those basic concepts that we all have in mind, and we all think in varying degrees that we apply in the discipline of security selection, security analysis. It is interesting when we go back to our roots in our thinking about these subjects, that we find sometimes there is more there than we had really realized lately. So, this morning I am going to address the question of intrinsic value. I think that is the Graham and Dodd expression. I think they created that particular term, and, of course, they always used it. This is a familiar term to all of us who have ever thought in value terms—every one of us who has ever fancied the notion that securities do get undervalued and overvalued in that marketplace where lots of silly, irrational occurrences are constantly operating.

AUTHORS' NOTE

Benjamin Graham and David Dodd introduced the concept of intrinsic value in their seminal work, *Security Analysis*, published in 1934. What might come as a surprise to some readers is that Graham and Dodd never provide a specific definition of *intrinsic value*. Rather, they discuss the concept in more general terms and illustrate their thoughts with specific examples. For Murray, intrinsic value is the estimate of the economic value of the company, as he states in the following paragraph.

What we are talking about when we use the term *intrinsic value* is this is our estimate of the economic value of a company, of an industry or of equity securities taken as a whole. We are talking about the quantitative and qualitative factors that support, define that intrinsic value, quantitative and qualitative factors, as the familiar expression. We know about lots of these, even at the University of Chicago, the home of efficient markets and where for generations they taught the notion that real security analysis was the fine public service, but not one that entitled you to income for providing it.

AUTHORS' NOTE

The debate surrounding market efficiency has always been a hot topic in the world of value investing. Market efficiency was pioneered at the University of Chicago by Professor Eugene Fama.[1] In simple terms, an efficiently priced security means that the market price equals the company's intrinsic value. Consequentially, there is no benefit from security analysis, and one will not earn excess returns (or income, in Murray's terms) from trying to determine a company's intrinsic value because the market price already reflects all available information.

It is security analysis, after all, that makes the market efficient, and because all of us have worked so hard at that process, we have brought any notion of value, any notion of market pricing, together. And you and I cannot possibly improve upon the market's capacity to estimate the future profitability of an investment.

AUTHORS' NOTE

Murray correctly recognizes that it is the cumulative hard work of all analysts in the marketplace that results in price equaling value. Consequentially, when price equals value, that security is efficiently priced.

I have always said to myself, "Roger, you surely were lucky to be born when you were.[2] You didn't know that the market was so perfectly efficient that you could not possibly, just by developing your skills as a security analyst, earn superior rates of return." One of the great advantages of ignorance on such matters may well be that you go right ahead and accomplish the impossible, and we have a room full of people here this morning with some of those same presuppositions.

AUTHORS' NOTE

Although Murray never accepted the efficient market hypothesis, he reluctantly acknowledged that the market had become more efficient over time.

If we have developed a series of techniques of valuation, we really can put our computer systems to work, and, with the application of sensible quantitative methods, we can identify securities that are in some sense mispriced. So what do many people do? As a minimum they say, let me devise a screen. I want to have a low ratio of market to book. I want to have above-average dividend return, and

I would like to have a low price earnings (P/E) ratio. Done all the time. And we have lots of studies, and it was absolutely fascinating that Gene Fama and Ken French just last year came up and told us you think there is something called the market line,[3] the higher the volatility of a stock, the higher the expected return. So all you need to know is what is the stock's beta coefficient,[4] and you could now tell whether that is possibly a high return; highly variable return; or a stable, consistent lower rate of return.

And how do you arrive at those conclusions? We know how. We all have our instruction in statistics, and we all know to get results with a high level of confidence, we have to have a lot of observations. So, what Fama and French[5] did in their most recent analysis was to take a couple of thousand stocks, 1963 to 1990—now you have the number of observations you need to reach a valid statistical conclusion. They concluded something that, interestingly enough, some of us thought we had known for fifty or sixty years, namely, that if you bought stocks on average at lower premiums of market to book value, you had a very good chance of getting superior returns.

Well, it was interesting because what this study said was, across the board, the volatility as measured by the beta coefficient is not the best clue. The best clue is an old friend of ours called the ratio of market to book. Fascinating. Both are so very interesting in our thought process about things like measurement of performance.

We have been thoroughly indoctrinated over the years that we want to be in that upper lefthand quadrant in that scatter exhibit of portfolio results. Where did we get the best return with the least variability in that return?

Now some people come along and say, "Really, you know, the variability factor is not the clue, and we can go back to a kind of an old-fashioned notion that what I really want is the best return, and unless I have a liquidity problem,[6] I really do not care very much about the extent of the variability in that return. Sure, I am used to having noise, random fluctuations in everything I measure in the capital markets, but I am not going to be distracted by them."

So these studies are under some serious question about the slope of our old friend the market line. But most of all, think about what these calculations represent. What they represent is averaging, averaging, averaging. Think about what we are interested in. What would you like to get your hands on in any one of the relationships? The answer is, you would like to get your hands on an outlier, the unusual case. That may be the clue for under- or overvaluation. If that is what you are after, surely, we should not get obsessed with average figures, central tendencies, which have skillfully and completely obliterated the differences from that central tendency. We talk nowadays about regression to the mean. Wonderful idea. We did not talk about it in those terms. What we said was, intrinsic value is a magnet in a rational world that pulls market price toward that intrinsic value. People are fundamentally thoughtful, analytical, rational. It may take longer, or it may happen quite soon, we will talk about that in our fourth session, but that intrinsic value is a magnet that is constantly pulling market prices towards it. And, if you prefer, you can call it towards intrinsic value or you can call it regression to the mean, which implies, to some extent at least, that the intrinsic value is the true, underlying, central tendency in the valuation of an enterprise, an industry or a class of securities.

AUTHORS' NOTE

Murray often referred to intrinsic value as a magnet that pulls price toward that value. The strength of the magnet determines how efficiently the security is priced.

When we look at all these kinds of measures and relationships, and we take them off the calculator, we have lost the precious ingredient. How much weight should I give to a low market to book? How much weight should I give to other of the variables that I am using? That is not in the statistical analysis. That is the application of seasoned judgment to calculate for this particular analytical problem what the weights ought to be in some meaningful sense.

I remember one time talking with Ben Graham, and we were discussing one of our favorite topics, which is that reported earnings[7] are generally a very biased estimate of the underlying events. We all know that the chief financial officer of a large public company has an assigned role. How do you maximize the value of the enterprise in the securities markets? We know how—reduce the variability of reported earnings—and we are talking about exercising all of the range of alternatives in generally accepted accounting principles (GAAP) to smooth, to adjust the timing of realization of gains and losses. And in this wonderful world, we can always think of two pictures, moving pictures of a going enterprise. The one is the underlying reality, the untouched photograph where all of the variations, and uncertainties, and disabilities, and mistakes, and misallocations of resources and effort are clearly visible. And then there is that other picture that that skillful chief financial officer has put together, wherever he has the choice. Let's smooth, let's show consistency, let's show a picture that is reassuring because it will command a better price in the marketplace if it presents that kind of a picture.

And now we live in a world where there are wonderful things that we can do. Let's just mention in passing that delightful practice of discontinued lines of business, and in a year like 1992 when you have got a special charge for your retiree health benefits, and the changes in the booking of income tax liability, what a wonderful opportunity to write down the value of that discontinued enterprise, set it aside, and from then on, that section or activity of the business disappears like magic. We will show you that nice ten-year performance of continuing businesses, and it is not long before everybody has really forgotten or lost track of that disaster along the way. Wonderful retouching of the photograph of this business across a span of time.

What do we want to know? As security analysts, we want to know, what is it really like? How did this management deal with this problem? How did they really do on acquisitions and divestments? What is the scorecard really like? If we want to smooth it, if we want to touch it up, we know how to do that. We are highly skilled at the fine art of averaging. Now, we do not need that friendly chief financial officer to do it for us with his particular biases. But one of the things we know is we have to live with that marketplace. What we have accomplished in security selection is all nothing but paperwork until we have actually transacted in that marketplace. So the market really matters. If you are winding up a transaction, that is where the final recording will be made.

So what if the prices and returns of a company are very volatile? It only makes a difference if you have a liquidity need. When I use the term *liquidity*, I am talking about that characteristic of an asset which makes it convertible into cash on short notice without material risk of loss. I am not talking about marketability. I am not talking about transaction costs. I am not talking about anything except liquidity in that sense.

If I have no liquidity problem in my long-term, long-time horizon pension fund or my educational endowment or in any of those areas, why should I care about the variability of returns? Well, I might like it. I might like it if I think many of those episodes are not reflecting fundamental characteristics of the enterprise but are simply reflecting the erratic behavior of decision makers in various kinds of environment. I say, gee, the wider the range of pricing, the greater the opportunities for me to enhance my total return.

AUTHORS' NOTE

As Murray points out, volatility is only a challenge if the investment holding period is time constrained. Downward price movement may provide a buying opportunity when price is less than intrinsic value, but the investor must have a high degree of confidence in her or his estimate of intrinsic value to exploit the price decline.

Let me just take the simplest example of all. I own an equity portfolio and I rebalance my equity portfolio relative to other types of assets periodically. I will add value across time. We have tested it many times, and the answer is, you certainly will by the simple act of rebalancing. Of course, as investment managers, we do not advertise this to our clients. We do our rebalancing nicely and quietly and happily, except an extra kudo or two in our performance measurement. But think about that process of rebalancing and how it works. You realize volatility is a good thing. What is not a good thing is, of course, nonrecoverable declines in price. When we say we can use variability and volatility across time, we are saying on the assumption that what is happening out there is not that the underlying ingredients of economic value are highly questionable, though we are talking about the pricing in the marketplace of what we have identified as real areas of economic value.

AUTHORS' NOTE

What Murray means by a nonrecoverable decline in price is when the true intrinsic value of the company ends up being less than the price paid for the investment. Benjamin Graham called a nonrecoverable decline in prices a permanent capital loss, which he believed was the primary risk in owning equity securities.

All right, think then about risk as it is conventionally described. We all know what risk is. It is the standard deviation of returns. We know that. That is what modern portfolio theory has taught us. Let me suggest for a moment, forget it. That is not risk. That is illiquidity, illiquidity. Will you get paid for accepting illiquidity? Of course, you will. You should expect to because there are always those people out there for whom liquidity is number one on the list of desirable properties, and if you as a broker/dealer are positioning that block of stock overnight, you are not interested in intrinsic value. You are interested in the liquidity characteristics. So I say fine. If you have liquidity problems and they are real, do not change the companies in your portfolio, just go out and buy or sell the contingent claims, options, and futures that hedge you against that kind of illiquidity, and go on about your business of owning companies that make sense in terms of their potential total return across time.

AUTHORS' NOTE

Modern portfolio theory defines risk as volatility, which most fundamental investors, Murray included, do not accept. As mentioned above, volatility becomes risk only when the investment is time constrained, and the investor is forced to liquidate the investment even though the current price is below the company's intrinsic value.

If you have no liquidity need—and we can think then about the growing defined benefit retirement plan, or we are thinking about the permanent endowment of a foundation or an educational institution—what do you really want to think about as risk? We know what risk is. You buy that company, and it goes down the drain. You are talking about . . . that is not volatility; that is nonrecoverable loss. It has occurred . . . we are not talking about what the price did. We are talking about what that corporate entity did, and the answer is, it failed. And we watch business failures all the time. Some are identified under Chapter 11, but some are just failures in an economic sense, in a meaningful sense. That's risk. Risk, we ought to think about as exposure to possible disappointment in that investment outcome. That is what we ought to be concerned about. That is risk in a meaningful term. Volatility is something, most of the time, we do not need the liquidity that we pay for in the form of sacrificed return, and if we do have legitimate liquidity needs, there is a market out there in liquidity which we ought to use.

AUTHORS' NOTE

Whereas modern portfolio theory defines risk as volatility, investors who base their investment decision on fundamental analysis and estimates of intrinsic value define risk as the possibility of permanent capital loss resulting from true intrinsic value being less than the price paid for the investment.

Let's think . . . let's turn our thoughts to this question. How efficient is the market? And I would like to have that first chart to look at for a moment. This is one of the least exciting charts that one could imagine. It's just taking a long look at the S&P 500. This line here is, of course, the real meaningful line. That is the stream of dividends, potential returns of ownership of equity securities. And when we talk about valuation and the ingredients of valuation, we will always be talking about either dividends or the capacity to pay dividends, and these are essentially interchangeable. Just take a look at the long trend this covers from the early fifties to the late eighties, and it gives you that picture of . . . sure there are some marvelous variations in that dividend stream, but they are nothing like the fluctuations in price.

AUTHORS' NOTE

John Burr Williams was one of the first academics to argue that a company's intrinsic value was the present value of all future dividends discounted backward for time. Williams developed the dividend discount model (DDM) to illustrate the process of discounting all future dividends as part of his PhD dissertation when he attended Harvard Business School. His full dissertation, titled *The Theory of Investment Value*, was published by Harvard University Press in 1938.

Let's look at those major price dips. If you go back there to the 1970s, and the market told us that the outlook for dividends was poor, well it was not one of the best periods of dividend growth, but it was far from a disaster. Take our worst market experience of the recent past, and there is 1974, what was the market forecasting? Prices are always a forecast, your best estimate of the future. Prices are always forecasting the expected outcome. How was it? Gee, dividend stream looked real fine and healthy. So, we say, wrong again. There is 1982 telling us that earnings and the dividends derived therefrom are not looking favorable. It is not the way it turned out. Our correction of 1987, in a sense, was a forecast that we had to revise downward, significantly, our expectations for the returns from equity investment.

AUTHORS' NOTE

Murray's comment that "prices are always a forecast" is an important observation. The stock market is a discounting mechanism, and the market price represents a consensus of investor expectations about the company's future financial performance.

How wrong can you be? You could be pretty far wrong, can't you? On this ratio scale, some of these fluctuations do not look as bad as we remember them so vividly if we were putting our judgments on the line in 1973/74. By my calculations, it was the most rapidly paced decline in equity pricing in our history. The rate of change was greater than even a comparable period in the Great Depression and what lay ahead after a nice period of growth in corporate dividends.

There are lots of different ways, I suppose, of measuring efficiency of anything we do. I think you are all familiar with the statistical calculation that if you have five or ten years of superior investment performance, it is not statistically different from luck or random fluctuations. If you really want to get enough observations statistically to demonstrate that it is something that we can call superior performance, just stick around for the next twenty, thirty, forty years or so, and we will then have enough data to raise the confidence level to the point that you would like to see.

I would like to look at now a different dimension. Let's have the second chart, which addresses the value of the dividend stream and some variations in that valuation. As you see, it does not matter a whole lot what discount rates we use, although we know that since the center part of this period encompasses very high interest rates, we would expect the value of the dividend stream to be relatively low. It is interesting, if we just take the roundtrip—1970/71 where this chart begins and 1990/91 where the chart ends—and we came out at comparable levels of interest rates, we came out at roughly the same relationship.

This is very comforting when you think of what we have been through in the last couple of decades. And what does it tell us? It tells us familiar economic relationships are still operating, and what you will find across time is even something as erratic as market prices will be responsive across time to the underlying economic realities. And so, we can say, if we go to work on our efforts to estimate with reasonable credibility intrinsic values, for the marketplace, for industries, for market sectors, and finally for individual companies, we have, in fact, a fighting chance of coming out somewhere reasonably close to that future outcome.

That is what we are after. We are after making forecasts that we could rely upon—forecasts of future earning power[8] of a company, an industry, or when we are looking at the S&P 500, we are probably looking at corporate America's earning power. I keep emphasizing that term *earning power* to distinguish it from reported earnings. Every once in a while, we will find an earnings report that is closely representative, in line with earning power. Three cheers. Most of the time, that is not what we are about to find.

In Murray's view, earning power is the level of cash flow the company can generate on average over a complete business cycle. It is the analyst's job to estimate the company's earning power, and that cash flow is used to calculate the company's earning power value (EPV). To be useful, earning power needs an estimate of what the company can earn consistently over time.

What this is telling us if we can derive anything from the history of economic relationships, which have an underlying logic and rational validity, if we can then find that we are right, the marketplace where we transact is not really off in some different world, it is not on a different planet, but is in that same marketplace where we are operating. We can begin to develop some genuine conviction about what a company in a meaningful sense is actually worth.

If we think always of that dividend stream as being what we are valuing—let's take just a set of hypothetical values and do some very simple arithmetic. Let's assume that American industry earns 13 percent on average net worth. That's in the ballpark of what we are familiar with. Let's assume that the payout is 50 percent of earning power. That says that the equity will then grow at 6½ percent a year. If we continue to earn the 13 percent on the growing equity, then we know that net income will keep right on growing at 6½ percent. Let's say that equity sells at twice book, then the dividend return will be half of 6½ percent, or 3¼ percent. Add to a 3¼ percent current dividend returns to the 6½ percent in underlying growth, we have a total return of 9¾ percent. If twice book equals intrinsic value, the multiplier, the multiple of earning power represented by this valuation is 15.4 times.

Let me replicate here Murray's math in the above paragraph. When Murray states that "American industry earns 13 percent on average net worth," he means that the average return on equity (ROE) is 13 percent. If corporations on average pay out 50 percent of their earning power in dividends to shareholders, then they retain 50 percent to fund growth, which means they can finance 6.5 percent growth (50 percent of 13 percent). Murray further states that the company's stock price is two times its book value (equity); then the dividend yield will be 3.75 percent or one-quarter the company's ROE (50 percent payout divided by 2× equity). If the 3.75 percent dividend yield is added to the annual growth of 6.5 percent, the implied total return is 9.75 percent, which is close to the historical return for stocks. The final comment is essentially a price-to-earnings (P/E) ratio calculation. Murray states that intrinsic value is 2× book value (equity) and that the ROE is 13 percent. Therefore, the P/E ratio is price (2× book value) divided by ROE, or 15.4x.

$$PE = \frac{2}{13\%} = 15.4x$$

I was able, after some years of training, to go through the course without ever using the term *price earnings*, reflecting the notion that there is probably no more useless term for decision making that has ever crossed the mind of man. If you start with the notion that pricing is erratic, the market is usually wrong or is wrong most of the time, what would I want to use price for? If all you use for earnings is what companies report, not the genuine underlying earning power of the enterprise, what you have is an erratic number divided by an irrelevant figure, and what do you expect to get out of that? So, I trained myself to talk about the multiplier—value divided by intrinsic value divided by earning power gives you that multiplier.

Now in that chart, just to keep you in focus on what that 15× multiple is, the scale on that chart for the S&P 500, if you look carefully, you realize is a 15 to 1 chart. So, in doing the chart, they did not talk about an equilibrium relationship of value to earning power, but because market prices tend to gravitate towards intrinsic value, it made pretty good sense to use this scale rather than another.

Now, we will be back, and we will revisit in these sessions the questions that those figures I used in my simple arithmetic illustration make any kind of sense. How should we look at them? We will be back to that one.

But let's take another look about . . . if we can be more accurate than that silly marketplace, what kinds of opportunities do we have? And I've got another chart, now that we can look at that tells us, of course, that the opportunities are really fantastic. This is real S&P 500, deflated to take out the inflation factor which gives us so much trouble in these longer-term figures, and there it is. What can you say in a meaningful way about the efficiency of the market forecasting of the future?

If that market were your employee with the assignment to make those forecasts, the answer is, there is only one reaction—you are fired. Here you see the extreme in disparities. I am not talking so much about the early period of . . . we could say, we used to be able to use the term *chaos*, but since chaos is now a technical development, we can't quite use that, but it is clear that the external factors were overwhelming any of the factors normally at work in financial markets as you can prove. That point there, I don't hesitate to remind you, was realized in June 1932—that's when I started work. The only handicap I had is, obviously, I did not have any capital, but you could say that, otherwise, I've lived on a one-way street. However, when I get into this lovely period after I am through of the deep undervaluation of the late forties, this reminds you of how deep that undervaluation was.

We came into that wonderful period of stability. Bond yields fluctuated between 4½ and 5 [percent] for high-quality bond issues, and the inflation rate for this decade was around 1.7 percent a year. And really, we had the new era, and we had lots of discussions about isn't it wonderful that the variability of share prices has been so greatly reduced, and stocks are obviously better investments because they have become more liquid. At a more . . . other things equal, obviously, a more liquid asset is worth more than a less liquid asset. Well, that was a splendid expectation, reflected there. Too bad we ran into all of those problems of the seventies and the early eighties.

When we sit here, and we talk about the inability of those who set prices with their investment management's decision to foresee the future, we say, gee, how could we expect one to anticipate the oil embargo or other factors contributing to a level of inflation the like of which we had never seen in our history? Who had the capacity to make an accurate forecast about the level of interest rates and those other ingredients? We would say, gee, I never expected to have the opportunity to sit down and read next year's *Wall Street Journal*, much as I would like to. However, the question is not a question of perfection, not a question of, can the marketplace or security analysts or any other entities involved in this process achieve perfection? The only question is, can you do better? Can you do better?

AUTHORS' NOTE

Murray outlines the fundamental challenges of doing investment analysis in a highly competitive capital market by raising the question, "Can you do better?" The statistical evidence is that it has become increasingly difficult to outperform the market, which suggests that the answer to Murray's question is no.

Let me tell you one story because I think it illustrates this point. Some of you are familiar with the Common Fund[9] for the Endowment of Educational . . . for Educational Endowments, we had started it. We had launched it with the Ford Foundation grant in 1971 that paid the cost of starting up the fund for the first three years. Comes 1973/74, college endowments were being withdrawn from the Common Fund. We had our annual meeting scheduled for September 24, 1974. You remember that the first bottom was on October 8, so this was really close. And we said . . . for our board of trustees sat there and said, this is a disaster. Look at what's happening to educational endowments. They are withdrawing, and they are withdrawing from our equity fund in order to liquidate. I said, we got to send a message. So we all got together, and I said, let me write the first draft. Everybody said, oh fine, fine, you write the first draft, and we will get together on the investment committee.

I wrote my first draft, and the committee got together, and you know what happened. "That language is a little bit too strong." I was talking about this being one of the rare investment opportunities to own equity securities that comes in a person's lifetime. Needless to say, my good colleagues and friends said, "We can't say quite that." We went through it, and when I saw the edited version, it had lost practically all of its real message.

So I came back, and I said, "I've got a proposition that you can't resist. Let me make the speech. Let me give the talk at the annual meeting. And the last paragraph will say, 'Remember, I am speaking for myself and among a bunch of educators. We believe in freedom of expression, so, I am not necessarily speaking for my fellow trustees.'" And what I said to my colleagues, I said, "Look, you can't lose. If it turns out that this was an absolutely dismal, disastrous kind of a statement to make and circulate to all of our participants and perspective participants, we will point to the last paragraph." So, see, you know, that oddball professor spoke for himself, not for the Common Fund. If it turns out right, we will say, here was the Common Fund's position at the market bottom.

I sold the bill of goods, and it was one of the most widely circulated documents that I had ever composed, as you could imagine, in that particular environment. And the other curious thing was I got invitations to speak all over the countryside in the fall of 1974. Why? Because you couldn't find anybody who would stand up and say this is . . . stocks are cheap. This is the chance of a lifetime. Go to it. Raise your equity exposure. Buy your head off. And when I said . . . I remember a financial analyst in Chicago had come to me and asked, "But can we not, can we not identify some fundamental principles that guide us in making estimates of fundamental economic value?" Dave Dodd always liked to use the word *appraisal*. The trouble with the use of that is that it has . . . you keep thinking of it in a legal sense, or even worse, you think about it in relation to real estate, wonderful example of a failure to use the whole array of economic analysis tools, principles, guidelines.

During the glory days on real estate equity investing, I used to sit there, and I had a silly question that I kept asking. Why is it that the cap rate[10] you use never seems to change? You tell me that the principal factor in real estate is location, location, location. Now you have just shown me eight office buildings in different locations, and somehow or other you come up with the same cap rate. And if you have used a lower cap rate, and given this, a higher value, it is because you have studied the mixture of leases, and you have found that there is a very high expiration rate over the next five years. And what we all know is that the earning stream will grow, and grow, and grow as those leases roll over. And I would ask that silly question.

Your forecast is then the replacement costs are going to stay firm or drift higher and that there will still be, in some meaningful sense, a shortage of good space so that on each rollover of those old leases, you are going to get significantly better terms. And I would say to them, you have made a forecast about the supply of office space anywhere around the country that you want to talk about, and you have made a forecast about the demand relative to the growing supply of that space. And I always got the same answer: The trouble with you, Roger, is you are trying to apply some elements of security analysis and the valuation of securities to real estate, and real estate is different. They were absolutely right. Real estate, indeed, has been different, to everybody's great distress.

But my proposition, of course, is I do not care whether we are talking about a real estate equity or I am talking about a company; the same elements that give that physical asset value in financial terms have to be the same. We are talking about the level at which the asset generates returns and the characteristics of that stream of returns across future periods. We are talking about putting together a picture of a company in business, in motion, subject to all the vagaries of political and economic factors. I am saying for this phase of the industry's history, or the company's history, we have a logical, carefully thought-out set of assumptions as to what the future may hold. And, of course, thank goodness, we do not have to be completely accurate on every one of our forecasts. If we were, of course, our portfolio would consist of a single, one, best asset.

AUTHORS' NOTE

Murray stresses that, because of the inability to determine with complete accuracy what the future will hold, the investor needs to build a portfolio with more than one security, which in effect is the benefit of diversification.

What we have said to ourselves is, "Yeah, we think we have done a thorough, careful job, but we like to have something called a margin of safety." If we think we have identified an undervalued market, undervalued industry, or an undervalued company, we would like to feel, well, if you want to use Murray's rule is 20 percent. If it is not 20 percent undervalued is best at least, I will go on to the next candidate. If it is not 20 percent overvalued or more in my best judgment, I am not going to eliminate it from my consideration portfolio.

AUTHORS' NOTE

Benjamin Graham introduced the concept of a margin of safety in the *Intelligent Investor*, which was published in 1949. The concept of a margin of safety is the recognition that the investor's estimate of intrinsic value will never be precise. Therefore, it is necessary to estimate a range around the estimate of value to provide a buffer that minimizes the risk of the company's intrinsic value being below the price paid for the investment, which would result in permanent capital loss.

We do not have to be perfect. All we got to do is do better than the marketplace does, and what we have looked at this morning are the exhibits, and we can properly say the marketplace—looking at the composite of all major American companies in the S&P 500—we are saying the market is like a stopped clock. It is right. It was right in 1985. It was right in 1973. It was right in 1955. Gee, when you think about those as being the occasions on which market prices got pretty well into line with intrinsic values, you will say that is not my idea of an efficient market. That is not my idea of an efficient allocator of real resources to real output. We ought to be able to do better. And I think the record is actually quite clear that when we do work at it, apply ourselves, we can, indeed, do better.

AUTHORS' NOTE

To Murray, market efficiency means that the price of a security always equals intrinsic value. He believed that volatility violates the notion that price always equals value and therefore refutes the market efficiency hypothesis. Richard Thaler proposed a different interpretation of market efficiency, which he calls *"no free* lunch." With his no-free-lunch concept, Thaler states that prices may not always equal value, but the errors are not systematic and therefore cannot consistently be exploited over time. A second consideration is that, between Murray's lectures in 1993 and the publication of this book in 2022, the market has become considerably more efficient, which, in a large part, is due to information being much more readily accessible to all investors, the dramatic decrease in the cost of trading online, greater technological resources used to aid in the analytical process, and a great number of more experienced investors.

I have a suggestion that has never, as far as I know, been adopted by a chief corporate financial officer. What they say is, you've got to have a bottom righthand draw that you can lock. Up on the top of the table, you will have those lovely financial statements that you turn over to your PR people to make the pictures and the text and keep the chairman really happy and delighted with everybody. But down in that locked bottom drawer, this is where you, the chief financial officer, practice security analysis. Nobody has better information, better sources, better ability to make the distinctions between underlying reality and the smooth touched-up presentation that the PR people use. Sit down and do that security analysis. Discussing it with senior executives of the company may be too risky. If you really have a strong message, maybe you had better keep it in the locked drawer until you have found that new position with a different company.

This isn't what people want to hear, and this is why the role of a good security analyst is the role of the skeptic, the cynic. The world is so full of fluff and imaginary developments, on both sides, both positive and negative, that you really have to keep sorting, sorting, sorting.

The other problem, clearly, that the security analyst faces, having come to his own best estimates of intrinsic value, is to say,

"Well, okay, I am ready to transact. But when I go to transact, I am out there, and I have to answer the question, how much of my best thinking is already in the price?" And we have all had the experience; we do our very best kind of analytical effort, and we get all done—I always gave my students on their final exam . . . I gave them an actual company to analyze making sure . . . but it was the Graham Manufacturing Company in Doddsville, Ohio, because if they had any inkling of what the real price was, I knew how it was going to condition their answer. So, question, you have done your analysis and you find out that the clock stopped at the right hour, and market price and intrinsic values are right within a very narrow range. The most difficult thing in the world for a good analyst is to put in the circular file a really good analytic job.

AUTHORS' NOTE

One of the big challenges of performing a security analysis in search of mispriced securities is that the analyst does not know if a genuine mispricing exists until after completing her or his analysis. And, as Murray notes, it is impossible to get the time back from those efforts.

What happens most of the time? You go back to the drawing board and say, gee, I could not have done all this work and not found a very attractive investment opportunity. I know I have done a better job on this than the brokerage company reports I have read and that I have talked to the key analyst. If I come out in the same place, I must have overlooked something. Let me go back. I am sure I can find some positive potential developments so that I am going to raise that intrinsic value well above market price, and I could go ahead and make this recommendation that I am so well prepared to deliver to the most skeptical kind of an audience.

It is terrible, but it is totally human that we become captives of what we think is our best thinking on any subject. It is very hard for us to step back and say, "You know, if my colleague over here had written that report, I would have yawned and told him to go back and try again. But when it is my report, I have great difficulty in stepping away from that."

So . . . well we have some better tools than we used to have. I can get the IBES[11] reports, and I can get a consensus of what analysts are forecasting, and I can do some very, very good, real fun kinds of exercises. What is happening to the number of analysts covering the stock? Very interesting statistic. Is the number increasing or decreasing? Is this being more intensively or less intensively followed by knowledgeable people? Now, let's look at what is happening to the forecast across time, and what is the range of the forecast? Perfectly simple, the wider the range, clearly the lower the level of conviction about the future, and that may be an opportunity.

AUTHORS' NOTE

We now know that cognitive diversity of participants increases market efficiency. Whereas Murray suggests that the wider the range of estimates indicates a lower level of conviction about the future, which may lead to an investment opportunity, the opposite is generally true. Although possibly not intuitive, the wider the range of estimates, the higher the level of price efficiency. We have learned that greater diversity in investor expectations leads to higher market efficiency, which is generally referred to as wisdom of the crowd.

What I really want to get at is, what are the expectations in price? Let me play them back. Ben Graham used to describe this as turning things inside out. Instead of my seeking to arrive at an intrinsic value based on my set of forecasts and assumptions, let me take the market's pricing and answer the question, what are the expectations contained in that pricing? Now, I am aware of the fact it may be fad. It may be fashion. It may be pervasive euphoria or panic, but when I deflate those expectations for a kind of a universal or composite set of expectations expressed in the marketplace, I have some guidelines. Now, I sit there, and I say, "Gee, that is the market's expectation. I think they are fundamentally wrong, and they are not wrong by a small margin. They are right up in that 20 percent zone. I think they are wrong in either direction by 20 percent or more." So, when I make my bet against the market consensus, I have got "a margin of safety" in my calculation, and there are the . . . that's my cushion;

that's my room for having made some poor or not well-informed or illogical assumptions.

All security prices are a culmination of a multitude of individual investor expectations. The analyst must understand what those expectations are if she or he wants to identify a mispriced security. Without question, estimating investor expectations is the toughest part of active investment management.

But when I sit down and say to myself, "What do I think the marketplace is going to think down the road?" I have a very simple but not highly academic approach to that problem. When you get up in the morning and you look in the mirror to put on some lip-stick or to get out the razor, say to yourself, "I don't know how to predict the market's behavior today, tomorrow, next week, next month, next year. I don't know what is going on in the minds of all of those people out there, some of whom I know quite well, some of whom I do not have the remotest idea of how their minds work. What is the thinking of that marginal participant in the marketplace that makes the difference in that market price stream?" Answer: "Remember, Roger, you do not know. You do not have any train-ing. You do not have any skill." You do not have any experience, except some bad experience that we have all had in thinking we knew how to estimate what was going on and what would be going on in the minds of this strange group, unpredictable group, a group that keeps changing all the time. Never have we had as much global inputs into that pricing mechanism all around the globe.

If you thought at one time that you could use the odd-lot[12] index—some of you may remember the days when we used the odd-lot index—what other odd-lotters net buyers or sellers of stocks. And when they were overwhelmingly buyers, you ran for cover; and when they sold, and, even better, when they sold odd lots short, these members of the public, you figured this was the buy opportunity of the decade. Wonderful. One of my favorite proj-ects for charting, studying. I could get a kind of a representation. What happened to me? What happened to that splendid indicator?

You do not see it anywhere, do you? It has no validity. It has no bearing. Look at the transactions—institutional large blocks, activity in contingent claims, international markets—you cannot find a sensitive indicator.

AUTHORS' NOTE

As we stated above, the markets are appreciably more efficient today than they were in 1993, mostly because of the dramatic increase in the number of professional investment professionals. In most situations, the consensus estimates have gotten more accurate over time, and thus it is challenging to find mispriced securities today.

I have still got one left. I do not know whether it is going to survive another round, but that is a very scientific test—the population of boardrooms in midtown Manhattan. If they are empty, think seriously about buying. If they are crowded, fall with tape readers and shore up your defenses.

But really, when I talk about such silly examples, you are getting the sense of the fact that we do not have a discipline. Those who are technical analysts say, "Oh no, oh no, we have got the answers." Just look at prices. We have looked at prices, and we know a lot about prices. Prices are independent of previous prices. Prices have no predictive power over future prices. You go through all of what we have done in quantitative methods, and we have identified what I call runs, and if you follow the runs, you will enhance the earning power of your broker and come up with little or no incremental returns.

Reading the prices . . . I used to have a technique for checking it when I was at the bank. I said I want to know about the outlook for interest rates. Obviously, I am going to talk to my guys in the bond department who are on the trading desk and have that intimate feel of the marketplace, and I talked to them. After a while, it did not take too long to learn that if I wanted to know what they thought, pick up the morning paper. It was all in the price, and they were telling me nothing different than what I could see on the table of prices—their time horizon, and it had better be. If you are going to be a market maker in Treasury securities by the billion, you had better not sit back there and talk about the implications of the new administration on deficit spending and the public debt. Let's get right down to a technical situation. This is where liquidity is the whole story.

Now let me close this morning with a question that I am going to put to you. In some parts of this world, some not unknown to all of you, there is an expression called "private market value"—a fascinating expression. I asked myself if, and we really ought to get Mario [Gabelli] to answer this, are we talking about intrinsic value dressed up, given a different label because it is more appealing to people if I talk about private market value rather than what some people think of as an unreal abstraction called "intrinsic value"?

AUTHORS' NOTE

Mario Gabelli introduced the concept of private market value with a catalyst as a measure of what an informed strategic buyer would pay for a business in its entirety in a private transaction. The 1980s was a period of active mergers and acquisitions, and this metric proved to be a valuable way to determine what a company would be worth to a strategic buyer or in a leveraged buyout transaction.

If I say to myself, how would I define *private market value*, I would say it is likely to be intrinsic value plus, potentially, a control premium because, by definition, being private I can turn over my business in jeans to a private entity, and I can use a longer time horizon than if I got those ridiculous analysts and shareholders out there giving me a hard time. So potentially there can be a control premium of value, and there may be a patience factor. We will talk about this. The greatest deficiency in the market's pricing of corporate America is its lack of patience. So maybe if we have it private, we have a better ability to exercise patience.

But there is one negative. I always like to be able to maximize the flexibility and effectiveness of a company by public financing of the enterprise, and I like to have access to the capital markets right at hand. I will even register those huge bond issues that I can take down in twenty-four hours, and I do not have to negotiate, enter into loan agreements, or any of those kinds of restrictive features. So I would take that as a subtraction. If private market value means intrinsic value, plus that control premium, plus that patience asset, minus market access, I say, "Okay, now I know what private market value is, and it is not a very exciting concept, but it may have a good deal of value in communicating to people who say, Do not give me that stuff about intrinsic value." The only thing that a company is worth is what you can sell it for in the marketplace, and that hidden assumption that market prices are accurate, precise, reflective underlying economic values.

So I will leave that for our next session. I want to give Mario a week or so to think it over, and when I take his name in vain on private market value, and I kind of shrug my shoulders . . . I think he is entitled to something approaching equal time—approaching equal time, but not exactly. Thank you all for your attention.

GABELLI: That concludes the formal part of our first meeting. Roger has volunteered to stay for as long as you would like to ask any informal questions, so we will do that either from here or just outside, whatever. So thank you. We will see you all next week, and those of you who can't join us next week, we will be more than privileged to get tapes to you privately.

11

LECTURE 2—INGREDIENTS OF MARKETS AND VALUE

(January 29, 1993)

GABELLI: We're again privileged to host our second in our series of four lectures on security analysis, and today the subject matter is the ingredients of market and value. Professor Murray last week threw down the gauntlet and suggested that intrinsic value was king, that private market value may have been cosmetically interesting but that it did not add much to the body of knowledge.

Today, before we turn the classroom over to Professor Murray, we'd like to and are privileged also to introduce Meyer Feldberg, dean of Columbia Business School. Before joining Columbia, he had a distinguished career at distinguished institutions, and it's hard for me to say these names: MIT, Northwestern, Tulane, and most recently was president of the Illinois Institute of Technology. Meyer Feldberg has put a great spark into a great institution, and he's going to make it even better for the balance of this decade and into the twenty-first century. And for those of you who went to Harvard, I'm sorry. Meyer Feldberg.

DEAN MEYER FELDBERG:[1] Thank you, Mario. I mean for us it's the Mario Gabellis and the Roger Murrays, in fact, that in many ways constitute the spark of the Columbia Business School.

My purpose today is to briefly introduce Roger Murray to this audience and, obviously, to the tape that is being made of this morning's presentation. Professor Murray is in large part responsible for the fact that, for over half a century, the principles of Graham and Dodd in value investing have been an important part of the Columbia Business School tradition. Mario's sponsorship of this lecture series is another link in this chain, and the Columbia Business School students; alumni, quite a few of whom are here today and work with Mario; and faculty who are here today are also testimony to the incredible viability and vitality of the value investing approach.

Professor Emeritus Roger F. Murray joined the school in 1956. He first served as associate dean and professor of finance, and subsequently became the first S. Sloan Colt Professor of Banking and Finance. In one of many demonstrations of the desire of those who know Roger to honor him, the professorship was sponsored by Bankers Trust, where he had previously held a senior position.

Taking over the security analysis seminar from Ben Graham, he also taught classes and supervised doctoral students in three major areas: security analysis, portfolio management, and capital markets. During his extraordinarily productive career with the school, Professor Murray was respected by all his colleagues, students, and administration as an instructor, as a faculty member, and as a friend.

Among the many honors bestowed upon him is a special tribute to Professor Murray's dedication as a teacher and as a mentor. Former students from the class of 1967, including Mario Gabelli, made a gift to the Columbia Business School last year to name the large lecture hall in Uris Hall in Roger Murray's honor. As one successful prodigy remarked, and I quote, "Professor Murray was able to bring to us an intellectual approach to life, and that in itself was a rare inspiration to people in the 1960s and those before and those who were lucky enough to be with him."

Please join me in welcoming Roger F. Murray.

MURRAY: It's nice to be introduced by such gracious colleagues, but you and I know the introduction doesn't take you very far. You've got to get to the substance quite promptly. So that's what we're going to do.

I'm not here to pick on the Value Line[2] this morning, but you may recognize this chart as coming from their service. They call it a forecast of the market for 1993. So let's kind of look at the ingredients. If you can read from your handout the equation here, you'll see that the first item is a trend line 2.4 percent a year, long-term secular growth. And then we come to the other factors which they have identified, and they are not too surprising—year-to-year change in earnings is a natural ingredient; year-to-year change in dividends, of course; and finally, on the negative side, a rise in interest rates is presumed to be negative for the stock market.

We look at charts like this all the time. And if we're not careful, we may even pay attention to them. Let me explain to you why this is an absolutely useless exercise. What are we doing? We're taking a span of years and you all know that 1932 bottom, the day Murray entered the financial community, and the Dow[3] was at forty years old, but he had no capital. If we use that whole span, obviously we'll get many more observations. And we all know at the heart of testing validity of a statistical calculation, the more observations the better.

Let's think about that for a moment. Of course, we ought to count what happened in the Great Depression, shouldn't we? Should we? How many of you anticipate a repetition of that unique and disastrous experience? How many of you have clearly in your mind that an oil embargo will surely be included in our next experience? Or cold war? Or any of the kinds of ingredients that went into this long span of years? And the answer is, by and large, history is not completely irrelevant, but it is not a reliable guide to the future.

Think back just a few years ago when we had a market correction, in 1987. Almost every business magazine you picked up did an overlay, and they overlaid the 1929 market break on the 1987 market break and showed you what the subsequent events were in the 1930s. Presumably, this overlay had some value in framing your expectations for the future. Remarkable exercise in, I call it, silliness. When you get into the silly season, we create all kinds of artifacts because it's easier to do that than to sit down and seek one's way through the factors that are going to affect the value of equities in the future.

So in the first place we might say that this forecast for 1993 is simply a statistical calculation of what might be the outcome if this pattern of market price reactions to all kinds of underlying events has some validity. Most of us, as we have been sitting down thinking about 1993, are thinking in terms of a whole series of macroeconomic developments that may be in the process of taking place.

Of the several ingredients, however, we can recognize that earning power and the slope of the dividend stream are indeed critical elements in the determination of intrinsic values across time. So that we will say earning power and dividend stream, and today we'll be talking some about the role of interest rates, the time value of money in determining the intrinsic value.

But the important thing that I would like to emphasize here is that the time frame used, one year's change, is an interesting observation. It's not entirely irrelevant, but when you buy that earning power stream, that dividend stream, and you make the outlay to purchase that stream, you are obviously making a long-term investment. You are making your judgment in terms of expectations over a period of time, and one year certainly is not the measure.

It's always interesting to think about what we can use. How about a seven-year time frame, where you are trying to identify the midyear, the fourth year of that seven-year time frame in the determination of intrinsic value. Where do I get those numbers from? Just from the reality of our ability to make credible forecasts of the future. We often think about the experience of an investment or the experience of a company over a market cycle. Well, we only know the duration of a market cycle in hindsight, but if one uses, in framing his expectation, a period like four years or thereabouts, there is a fair chance, no certainty, but a fair chance that that span will have encompassed enough of a range of macroeconomic and market factors to be useful. So if we think in terms of that kind of a time horizon, we've got at least a reasonable chance of coming up with some observations that make sense.

The other observation in looking at any of these long-term time series, observations about, you see them all the time, historical price earnings ratios. You've heard it recently, haven't you? These price earnings ratios in the marketplace in 1993 are not high relative to historical price earnings ratios. Always a very interesting observation because the next questions is, What historical observations? Are you talking about the 1960s when bond yields were 4½ and 5 percent, the inflation rate was well under 2 percent a year, or are you talking about the history of the late 1970s, when all of those factors were drastically different?

I have said, indeed, as a client to investment managers, please do me a favor, never make the statement in relation to your portfolio management that it has something to do with historical factors. That's not an answer to anything. What we want to know is, and what we may be able to get some guidance for in history, What are the implications in the determination of intrinsic value of the best expectations that we can frame about? Growth, the earning power, growth in dividends, and the interest rate factor that we are going to apply in the valuation of that stream.

So let's turn now to a second simple kind of an expression, which is an old familiar statement. Let's think for a moment about an indefinite time span by the decade. Let's think in terms of equity securities of major established companies. Let's talk about a kind of a weighted average of corporate America. Let's try and arrive at a sensible M, multiplier, the ratio of intrinsic value to earning power, and see how we get at it and how we come out. D is our old friend, dividends. We're talking about dividends or the capacity to pay dividends. We are not quibbling over the desirability of retaining earnings in a period of high profitability and rapid growth instead of paying them out and selling shares to finance that profitable rate of growth.

So let's talk about D, dividends, as the capacity to pay a return in current dollars to shareholders, reflecting the earning power of American business or of an industry or of a company. K is our discount rate or expected return, however you like to express it. What do I expect? What do I demand if I am going to be an owner of what we call illiquid assets, variable assets?

What we know, that if the earning stream is growing, we are going to use that expected growth as an offset to the expected return, talking about current earning power at the current time. So we now have the ingredients, and I have used some illustrative figures, not necessarily a forecast but maybe somewhere in the range of intrinsic value.

Let's assume the payout of earning power is about 50 percent. So, we have 50 cents of dividend for every dollar of earning power. Our discount rate, our expected return, is 10 percent, and we'll talk about that a little bit more. But I really don't need to figure that out for myself because I can get a prospectus of the Gabelli Equity Fund and the president tells me that his expectation is that he will pay shareholders 10 percent a year in the form of dividends and capital gains. And so far, he's been able to do it. In any event he has given me that as a reasonable, responsible expectation, and I have some additional support, happily, for that same order of magnitude.

Growth rate, 6 1/2 percent. Where does that come from? It's not necessarily history, although we can find some periods that consistently approximated such a level. What we're talking about, as in that shorthand example I used last week, if you earn 13 percent on net worth and you pay out half of it and invest the other half, and you continue to earn 13 percent on the total equity, the equity will be growing at 6 1/2 percent.

It's not unreasonable if we assume some simple factors. Let's say that the workforce grows somewhere around 1 1/2 percent a year, and let's say that productivity output per hour is growing somewhere around 1 1/4; we have a 2 3/4 percent long-term trend of real growth. And if you add to that an inflation expectation of, say, 3 3/4 percent on the average, we have our total of 6 1/2 percent.

What we are after here is some long-term trends that will be factors in long-term earning power rates of growth. If we go back again to our 10 percent expectation, we can say we've got some pretty good evidence that in the 1990s the basic interest rate is right around 3 1/4 percent. If we add to that basic interest rate our inflation rate of 3 3/4, we have reached the conclusion that bond yields ought to be around 7 or 7 1/4 for AAA corporate bonds.

You notice two things about this calculation. Number one, I don't use a ridiculous statistic like the Treasury Bill rate, which has that high component of a liquidity premium. I don't use government bonds, because I know they have an income tax advantage at the state and local level. Really talking about a stream of riskless long-term returns as exemplified in a low-risk corporate obligation.

If, then, I can anticipate a basic long-term interest rate around 7 1/4, what should I expect as a long-term basic expected return on illiquid assets like equities? Well, my premium is 2 3/4 percent. Where did I get that from? I derive it judgmentally. I say I believe in the environment that lies ahead. We have a number of factors working on that required return or expected return. On the one hand, the explosion in corporate debt in the 1980s greatly reduced the quality consistency of earning power. Acting in the opposite direction, we can see that international competitive factors and many domestic factors have put tremendous pressure on corporate enterprise to exercise more careful control over expenses, to lower break-even points, to reduce operating leverage in the corporate enterprise. So we have factors working to enhance the quality in some meaningful sense of corporate earning power, and we have, as we can see, both positive and negative factors at work.

Part of our analytical task in making a forecast about the future, about the intrinsic value of a company, has got to be the best exercise of judgment about those factors that are at work and new factors that are coming along.

One of the observations that we make regularly is corporate earning power is chronically overstated, chronically overstated. Just think about what happened to the price level in the United States in the last twenty years. Think what happened to the value of productive capital assets as measured any way you like but thinking of it in terms of replacement value. It is absolutely clear that having gone through that kind of a period of widespread and pervasive inflation, the owners of corporate business must have had huge gains in the nominal value of their fixed assets. Therefore, when companies liquidate capital assets to move the location of the business, to rearrange their production capacity, to do all of those things, we will see large nonrecurring capital gains on capital assets.

Maybe I've been reading the wrong financial statements, but as I look over the financial statements for the last decade or so, what do I find? I find write-downs. Restructurings never give rise to changes coming from the change in price level. It's abundantly clear, is it not, that what American business has called depreciation, using up of the economic value of a capital asset, has been grossly understated.

What have they missed? They've sat around and let accountants using historical cost bases, seeking about the physical life of capacity, saying, "No problem, a building like that is good for twenty-five years or forty years or some other figure." And what has been the reality? The reality has been that you had to close that plant and build a new one. Maybe it was environmental problems, maybe it was plant layout, maybe it was the equipment in that building.

In any event, what have we been doing? We have been eating capital losses on corporate capital assets in huge quantities in spite of the fact that we went through the longest, most sustained inflation in our corporate history.

Or let's just take the current discussion. The FASB[4] says you've got to recognize the obligations that you have incurred for healthcare for retirees. Those commitments, in most instances, are just as real and clear and explicit as the obligations incurred in the adoption of a defined benefits pension plan. For a long time, we've been recognizing the pension liabilities as they are incurred and now somebody says, How about it? And the answer is, of course, there is no distinction in a fundamental sense between the pension benefits and the healthcare benefits.

As a retiree of Bankers Trust Company, every month I have deducted from my pension $20, which pays my full Blue Cross/Blue Shield extended range of benefits for myself and my wife. Twenty dollars! Really a pleasure. Do I know I am getting a benefit? You bet I know I'm getting a benefit. You bet I know that this is a cost, if that old mortuary table doesn't get me first, the benefit is going to continue for an extended period and that was a commitment that they made to me thirty-five years or so ago.

Again, what are we doing? What are we doing? We're doing all kinds of things. The discontinued business gimmickry that I mentioned last time in which we are trying to put the best cover on that financial statement that the ingenuity of man can devise.

So when I'm thinking about long-term earning power and I'm thinking about rates of growth in that, I'm trying to think as best I can. I'm trying to think about the underlying reality, talking about economic value in a meaningful sense, and I'm saying to myself, really, when I take a look at those splendid ten-year statements in the back of the annual report, I really have to say to myself, I ought to go back and accrue that health cost for retirees all the way back through the years in which that commitment was made and those liabilities were accruing.

For every write-off of capital values, I really ought to go back and restate the capital consumption allowance, the depreciation item in all of those previous periods. Now, I don't know whether you've ever tried to do this. I've tried and I'll give you my best judgment. Don't try. It defies the ingenuity of man when you are simply working with the published financial statements to go back and recast, recalculate rates of growth and the levels of profitability.

What can you do? Obviously, you can think about the qualitative characteristics of financial expressions of earning power, and you can say to yourself, if I am analyzing a pharmaceutical drug company, oh happy day! I don't have to really worry about depreciation because the fixed asset account is trivial. The big asset is, of course, completely intangible, off the books, new products in the process of development. And since the write-offs, the expending of this capital asset in the form of research and development expenses, is always current, I really don't have to worry about that particular aspect. But I needn't add I'm not home free on pharmaceutical companies because I'm still trying to estimate the life span of important drug products. And every time I turn around, I find that some products are being obsoleted more rapidly than others. Some of the patents expire, and I sell generics and make out just fine. Others, not so.

What we're talking about and what so often we forget about is the obsolescence factor that is at work in almost every activity that you can think of. It's not only variable as between industries and companies, it's variable across time. And so we are trying to deal with a relatively unstable factor in the forward estimation of earning power in a true sense.

When we go from earning power to dividend payout, what we know is dividends are paid in cash. The payout of dividends in relation to cash flow, preferably free cash flow, is much more stable than those silly statements that companies make about payout in relation to reported profits.

We know you don't pay cash dividends out of accruals. You pay them out of just plain cash. So when we think about the dividend policy question, which we have to, we have to equate that payout with cash flow, not with reported earnings.

But when we go back to look at the corporate structure, what do we say about retained earnings? If we are thinking clearly, I submit, we are saying that retained earnings are equivalent to a fully subscribed preemptive rights offering made on behalf of all shareholders.

We don't always think about it in these terms. If a company comes to market with a new share offering, we talk about dilution. Because what I'm saying to you here is every dollar of retained earnings is a quote, "potential dilution," if you want to think in those terms. Returned earnings are not a free good because we analysts are going to look at rates of return on net worth, on returns on total capital. Every penny of return: retained earnings is an addition to that capital base.

This is very interesting, and this is one of the reasons to use dividends or the capacity to pay dividends rather than earnings in arriving at an intrinsic value. The problem is very clear. There is slippage in the capital budgeting process, in the process of deciding what to pay out and what to retain.

One of the nice terms developed in the field of business finance that I like very much is called the agency problem. To me, I'm sure that many of you . . . we shareholders . . . theoretically elect directors to choose the management of the enterprise. While we know this isn't real, we know that the management of the enterprise selects the directors, and it gets us cheerfully to ratify that process through a wonderful vehicle called the proxy system. But you and I know that there is abroad in this world a notion that the larger the company, the higher the salary. The number of people you supervise is presumed to have some implications to the level of responsibility that should be rewarded.

Also, there's something you might think of as kind of a social factor at work. As a chief executive in my line of business, I know this business like the palm of my hand. I've been at it, we've been successful, we're profitable, but as I look down the road, I don't see in that marketplace significant opportunities for further expansion. Along comes one of my able eager experts on profit planning and long-range strategic planning for the enterprise and he tells me, "Look, Murray, with your ability at decision making, with all you've learned here in corporate finance and business management, all of those skills, you can just as well apply them to this other line of business and there will be a synergy between these two activities."

And I say, "Tell me again about that synergy? This looks like a totally different product line, different markets." And that fine young man with a good vision of his future says, "But, President Murray, you provide the synergy. Your decision-making process, your organizational skills are by definition readily transferrable to an additional line of business."

So let's keep the payout ratio low, let's use those reinvested earnings to diversify. A splendid word. To diversify our lines of business. You've all been through this. You've heard those presentations. This will balance, this will give us diversity, this will give us these special benefits, we use common distribution channels, or we've got the right position in Western Europe, or whatever all of those arguments are. And then a few years later you've had the experience where these same people come back and tell you they're doing a great thing for you as a shareholder because they are eliminating these activities that do not fit into our basic strategy.

And unless you go back and dig out those annual reports, and you read the two rationales, and you observe that they're signed by the same people, you think, I ought to be grateful to these decision makers twice. Once, when they had the foresight to broaden the scale and potential of our business and once again when they were the hard-nosed guys who bit the bullet and cut us back to our central areas of strength.

It's hard for a good chief executive officer to raise the payout rate even though the reinvestment opportunities are limited, and it would make more economic sense. Fortunately, though, without increasing the payout ratio in a manner which identifies you as a nonconformist, you can accomplish somewhat the same result by buying in shares.

The classic story, of course, was Exxon. You remember when they ventured into Reliance Electric and even started a little start-up venture capital and the business equipment and things like that, and after they had taken their bath, what did they do? Bought shares, bought shares, bought shares, bought shares.

As the alternative, their earnings retention in relation to the borrowed potentials of their economic activity was clearly excessive in relation to the investment opportunities that they could identify rather than go off in unexplored areas in which their competence and expertise was distinctly limited. They, in effect, unwound the retained earnings with the subscription on behalf of all shareholders to new shares and you cancelled it out by buying the shares back, leaving you with a fighting chance of maintaining at the rate of return on equity.

So we can identify some financial corporate structure decisions. We can identify some qualitative factors. That wonderful feeling that comes over a successful business executive that the capacity of himself or herself and colleagues is hardly even tested by present scale and scope of activity.

In a way, what we're talking about from the standpoint of intrinsic value is the dividend payout, the capacity to pay dividends, or the ability to earn on the new shares constantly being issued in the form of retained earnings. It's one of the things that we need to examine very carefully, and a company that's consistently increasing its capital base without a demonstrated capacity to earn at it has got to be worth less than one that is run as a spare enterprise in terms of the use of shareholder capital.

Let's turn now to a look at some historical rates of return. Very familiar to all of you, but when you take a little time on these numbers, they're really absolutely fascinating. We took care of standard deviation last week, the measure of illiquidity in these types of assets. We also defined risk, exposure to possible disappointing results.

Let's just take on the long look, called here modern times, 1945 through 1991. We'll take the broadest measure like the S&P 500, showing a standard deviation of 16.6 percent over that long period of time. That, I submit, is a measure of illiquidity. Many periods like that. But it's all in there. This is net of all of the disappointments.

Don't tell me I have to have a risk factor for disappointments. It's already in there. That's what I got after eating all of my mistakes over that long span of time.

All right. If I look at large cap, higher return on small cap, less liquid? Yup. That's exactly what we know. Or take emerging growth stocks, a new category that we're developing nowadays. And we say yeah, there's a case to be made for catching companies in their early phases of growth and development. They're going to be less liquid.

Go down here to venture capital. Look at that low liquidity on venture capital. Of course! That's what I always knew. I would enter that venture capital partnership; I didn't have the remotest idea of when I was going to come out because it would all depend on whether that IPO market blossomed and bloomed. And if it did, my holding period was fairly short; if it didn't, it turned out to be quite long. And there is a good deal of question about what that time span is likely to be.

In fact, if we turn over here to the last ten years, now the return was less, the illiquidity was still high. We went through in the last decade, we went through some real dry spells in the IPO market. This figure, of course, would look a lot better when we're able to add 1992 and some part of 1993.

But let's look again at some of these long-term relationships. They're extraordinarily sensible; the T-bill rate very slightly exceeds the inflation rate. That's a consistent relationship, it's logical, makes good sense, it's good economics. Indeed, people use the expected T-bill rate as a useful forecast of the inflation rate. So we expect that relationship to hold.

Here are corporate bonds returning as expected, a higher rate of return than riskless government securities.

U.S. farmland. Boy, just tell me what the time period is if you want an example of the endpoint sensitivity problem. There it is in its most acute form in the long history of farmland.

And, incidentally, in looking at these orders of magnitude, this is not a good way to measure. If you start in 1945, you start at a time when financial assets were cheap and equities were undervalued, and you terminate at a time when, you could put your own expression on it, equities are fully valued or fully priced or maybe overpriced.

So we don't pay too much attention to the observation of 11.8 percent. It doesn't say automatically now I know, Murray, that your 10 percent rate is too conservative in some sense given the future. The other things, of course, about this are that all commercial real estate has very high liquidity. I won't ask you to believe that, not even for ten seconds. But this is one of the problems when we don't know how to measure changes in prices. And let me tell you about the last decade of good returns, pretty good returns, with a very high level of liquidity applicable to commercial real estate.

Just in passing, we see some international calculations here that have become quite relevant. When you look at emerging market equities, we don't have enough data for any useful calculation. Most of us would expect that that return would be potentially significantly higher.

Just a couple of things to note about the equities. In the long term, we've got that pattern. The size factor, as we talk about it in terms of efficient markets. There is a small cap premium, presumably, perhaps. What we see is just what we expect: that those annualized returns rise with a diminution in the size of the company as measured by the market value of its capitalization.

Or look over here for this decade. What happened? We all know what happened when we lived through this and along about June, what was it, June 19, 1983, when the small cap market peaked and started on its own private bear market. We've got all kinds of explanations of this. The one I don't hear is a simple flow of funds factor in that experience.

Along there in the early eighties we came to the start of a huge wave of indexing. Every time an actively managed portfolio was converted into an indexed portfolio, the cash flows were favorable to large cap rather than small cap. If you look across actively managed portfolios, you'll find that there's a tendency of the size of holdings to be more equal, and certainly there is not a tendency for them to reflect the market cap of those individual companies.

So if you look simply at the transactions, when that active manager turns over the California Public Employees' Retirement System (CalPERS) portfolio of a few billion, you sell across the board somewhat related to an equal division. You've got forty stocks; you've got roughly 2 1/2 percent, not exactly in each. You turn around and you take exactly the same number of dollars and you now market-weight it. That transaction on that day, I submit, had an effect on the relative demands and supplies of shares in the marketplace.

If you do this in large amounts persistently over a long period of time, will it have some marginal impact? I don't have a good—a good study on that subject, and I haven't found anybody who was really excited about doing it, but I submit that it may be one of the factors at work that was favorable to large caps relative to small caps measured in terms of the demand for institutional pension fund holdings.

Other factors. Of course, we know that the recession impact is present here. We know that the change from a pervasive inflation to a disinflationary economy and a decline, significant decline, in that basic interest rate, all of that was favorable to what we might describe as quality growth companies. And that would include major pharmaceuticals and, in this case, it included major food, tobacco purveyors, and the like. And so that was clearly a factor in our framing of the future.

It seems to me that we can quite logically agree among ourselves that because of the greater illiquidity of these smaller and emerging growth stocks, we will expect, we will anticipate a higher average rate of return, and this pattern of the last decade is not a valid forecast of the future which we should employ in framing of our expectations.

As we look at this long history, one of the things we know for sure is that prices and price behavior are not forecasting in any meaningful sense. What they are doing is reflecting those fundamental, underlying characteristics that we are addressing when we are thinking in terms of the intrinsic value. Prices, we say in very general terms, are independent. They do not have inherent in them or in their behavior predictive values of the kind which we need.

What do we need? There aren't any shortcuts. We need to be right back there. What about the earning power of American industry, of American companies?

How should we try to frame our expectations about that future? We can pick up some crumbs of wisdom from experience if we know how to use it. At the time of the 1987 break, I said to people that there's some similarities with the 1962 break. Their eyes glazed over. Gee, they weren't managing money in 1962. They didn't have that experience. They didn't remember that it took almost twelve years before those wonderful stable food stocks got back to their overvaluation in 1962.

There are some characteristics, some trends that we can learn from history. What we know is the mind of man has an extraordinary capacity to rationalize all kinds of things. We go through periods when conglomeration of industry is the magic solution. It's not as though we hadn't been through that before and identified many of the reasons why it doesn't work. We go through periods of divestment when we try and get our act together, and then we go into long periods of time when acquisitions are clearly the magic formula. And we rationalize these with wonderful imagination and ingenuity so that, in June 1983, a small cap market had still an unlimited potential.

And by the same token, in October 1990, the discussion was what happened to the small cap effect? We've been sitting here, we small cap guys have been sitting here taking this punishment for seven years. Every time they got cheap, our enthusiasm increased, and all they did was get cheaper. Because now the world has discovered that you need, in this kind of an uncertain environment, in recession, all of those kinds of problems, you've got to have a broad product line, and you've got to have that internal diversification of the enterprise, you've got to find and identify new avenues, you've got to do all of those kinds of things that we've tried lots of times before.

And what's so fascinating about this, if you look at large periods across a span of time, really, there aren't that many brand new, unique fads or waves of thought processes that invade financial decision making. Many of these we have seen before, and we can in that respect get some value, learning from history. But if we're not careful, we tend to get captivated. We try to resolve these questions by analogy. They all . . . this has some points of similarity to a previous episode, and I will apply to this episode what happened in the previous episode.

We come back to that question: Is this not different? And if we do our homework and our analytical effort—of course, it's different. There are some fundamental relationships at work, simple as the time value of money. A liquid asset is worth more than an illiquid asset. There are strategic decisions that can be made in the planning of a company or an industry or, indeed, even in corporate America in the large that are positive, and some are negative.

Our task in trying to identify the real essence of value we describe as intrinsic value is to try and take account of all or as many of these factors as we can possibly analyze and digest. One of the things we know about forecasting is forecasting is difficult. It's especially difficult when you try to forecast the future. We think about that, I'm sure that's the way Yogi Berra[5] would say it, but what are we doing? We're trying to appraise the probabilities. And as we showed in our chart of the long history of market behavior, there's so much opportunity. There are such gains to be made from being less wrong that we don't have to say we are going to develop the techniques, the methods, the discipline that give us certain answers. We're not going to do that no matter how thoughtful, careful our analytical process, no matter how valid our reasoning.

But one thing is sure, and this is the word I like to use, discipline. Can we apply that discipline to a carefully thought-through, analytical process to our investment decision making? And, of course, we can. No short cuts. We're talking about working harder. But I think what we see is the potential for being right on occasion, but most of the time we're being significantly less wrong than the world around us, it's a tremendously rewarding prize.

Murray was one of the first business school professors to impress upon his students the need for rigorous, disciplined analysis. In his comments, Murray also acknowledges that the process of identifying mispriced securities was getting harder, which, in effect, means that the stock market had gotten more efficient.

Next week, we'll turn our attention to some individual companies and take a look at some of the processes relative to, not just at the field of equities taken as a whole, but individual companies. Thank you.

GABELLI: You should be aware that Professor Murray suggested that he would like to continue, but I have to cut him off at an hour and a half. This is a modern classroom, but the concepts are fairly fundamental and very basic.

In addition to discussions of valuations and techniques, the concept of agency problems comes right home to us all the time, so that our analysts want to become portfolio managers before they become analysts, Roger. They want to go directly to the step of losing money without learning the disciplines.

We also, Professor Greenwald, this is also one time in which we've had eight candidates for the master's program that are getting paid to attend the lectures as opposed to paying as they do. So we're delighted, and maybe we can get some feedback from some of the students on the whole subject of corporate governance.

The purpose of these lectures and these discussions is called valuation, but we might also, in light of what goes on in the world like American Express, General Motors, and so on, the whole subject of corporate governance and poison pills and various proxy processes are also fascinating subjects, but for another time.

Today, thank you, thank you all for joining us. We'll see you next week.

12

LECTURE 3—EQUITY PRICING
AND CAPITALIZATION RATES

(February 5, 1993)

REGINA M. PITARO:[1] I'm Regina Pitaro of Gabelli Asset Management Company, and I have the privilege this morning of introducing Dr. Murray to you.

Back in 1966, our chief investment officer, Mario Gabelli, took a class at Columbia Business School and it was called Security Analysis. In this class, Professor Murray taught the Graham and Dodd method of security analysis. This approach takes the view that the market's pricing of securities is often based on faulty and irrational analysis, and that the price of the security only occasionally coincides with the intrinsic value around which it tends to fluctuate.

Our firm, Gabelli Asset Management Company, was founded in 1977, and we have used the Graham and Dodd principles of fundamental security analysis to achieve 20 percent returns in the stock market for the past fifteen years.

Another famous Graham and Dodd disciple is Warren Buffett. He parlayed this knowledge into superior returns for his shareholders, who were the public shareholders of a company called Berkshire Hathaway, and he is also personally among the top ten in the Forbes 400.[2]

This is Graham and Dodd's *Security Analysis*, and this has been the investment bible for over fifty years. This textbook invented the profession of financial analysis for investment.

Back in 1988, Professor Murray coauthored the fifth edition of Graham and Dodd's *Security Analysis* and, when that came out, because it was such an important event for our firm, we were privileged to host a dinner[3] for Roger Murray. Sixty people attended. They included former students; Wall Street research analysts; other money managers, such as Lee Cooperman,[4] who was a student and a classmate of Mario's; and just plain fans of Roger Murray.

Roger's biography is stellar. In addition to his academic experience, he has managed investment portfolios at Bankers Trust. He has chaired the CREF[5] finance committee. He was a trustee of firms such as Alliance Capital Management, Putnam Investments, and the Common Fund. He was the public director of the Chicago Board Options Exchange. He is the founding director emeritus of the IRRC, that's the Investor Responsibility Research Center. He was a member of the president's task force on aging, and he is also the originator of the IRA, the whole concept of the individual retirement account. Thank you, Dr. Murray. Every time you make a contribution to your IRA, you can think about him.

It would take another ten minutes to simply list all of the stellar accomplishments of Professor Murray's. So we have to move right along and begin the lectures.

To date, we have heard two different lectures. The first was entitled "Value and Price." The second covered the ingredients of markets and value, and both were exceptionally well done. Today, we are about to hear Professor Murray discuss equity pricing and capitalization rates. So it's my distinct privilege to introduce to you, Roger Murray.

MURRAY: Thank you and good morning. We are going to visit an old and familiar area this morning and that's this total process of pricing financial assets, and we're going to look at the special case of equity securities in that process.

And if we look at this first chart that will be coming on of stock prices, it has some interesting information for us. To too many of you, there's nothing terribly exciting about that kind of a chart. Let me explain to you why it is an absolute gem. That trend line is a least squares calculation of the logarithms of the prices, a log least squares trend-line calculation. What's so great about that? It is the only way you can eliminate endpoint sensitivity[6].

We looked at some charts at one of our previous meetings, and what we have to say is well, those figures are kind of high. They are distorted by the fact that we started to measure at a low level of the market, and we finished measuring at a relatively high level. Here is the technique for eliminating the problem of endpoint sensitivity.

Now, it makes a better chart for us to get a long view of market prices. It eliminates the distortion created by running the line from point A to point B. But the other thing that it does for us is to give us some true perspective about variation around a trend. A central tendency, calculated in this case over the period from the late 1880s up to the 1980s, it works out to be 3.8 percent per annum price appreciation from the ownership of equities exclusive of dividends. The interesting thing in looking at the variations around that long trend line is that, when we look at the variations, we find that they are fairly persistent. This is not a line that simply vibrates up and down around the trend. We find that indeed there are significant periods of relative consistency and stability. Do we say, gee, those were the years that we all loved? And, of course, we are talking about the 1960s, moderate interest rates, an absence of inflation, 1.7 percent per annum in the consumer price index for a decade or so in there, and most of that is a distortion in our pricing measurement.

We can almost say we had a period of substantially no inflation and, if you go back to the period before the exciting 1920s, you have another period again, an absence of inflation. It's a kind of reminder, isn't it? Inflation is probably the most important single factor in the valuation of equity securities. We all say equities are obviously a good hedge against inflation. They certainly are. You and I would recognize that, if we own a company, that can make its way in the full range of economic activity; inevitably the value of that ownership will reflect changes in the price level but with a very appreciable lag.

We know this extremely well from our very fresh experience. Our inflation problem is of the 1970s, and that was not one of the pleasant, comfortable years for equity investors. In fact, it was a dismal period for equity investing; comes the time when we pass from consistent, strong, inflationary pressures to what we called in our terminology disinflation. Comes disinflation, comes the related moderation of interest rates and, all of a sudden, we find that equities produce probably the highest consecutive years of returns since we've been able to measure capital market returns with reasonable accuracy.

AUTHORS' NOTE

Interest rates in the United States declined significantly between 1981 and 1993. Equity valuation increased dramatically because of the lower discount rate, which resulted in strong stock performance during this period.

Brings us back, doesn't it, to the fact that too often we look at the stock market and we look at the market in securities as though it had a life of its own. It doesn't have a life of its own. It is a mirror reflecting underlying economic and financial events. Will there be a lag between the underlying events and their reflection in capital markets? Of course. You and I sit there as hopefully we all did and said, "Ah, the real problems of inflation are behind us. We're entering into a new period in which that's not going to be the principal problem for us to contend with." Fine, how long will it take for that sea change in the economic environment to be reflected in the pricing of financial assets? The worst the experience has been, the longer it will take for people to rethink and reorient their decision making to reflect the new environment.

It's a typical good news, bad news story. It's good news to know that there will be a change. It's bad news to know it will be very hard to tell when, and to what extent, that will take place. What that tells us, I think, as fundamental analysts, is that we need to think our way carefully through this process and be patient. Be patient. Patience is a very, very scarce supply in the American economy anywhere you turn and certainly in the equity securities market.

It stands to reason, if you can supply something that is very, very scarce and is not generally supplied by others, you will be able to negotiate a good price and a good return for that scarce commodity.

Let's think about some of these questions in terms now of an individual company and, for this purpose, I'm going to use an old friend, I would say an intimate friend called the Xerox Corporation. When I was elected to the board of Chemical Fund in the late 1950s, there was already in the portfolio a company called Haloid, from Rochester, New York. I've kind of grown up with Joe Wilson, the chairman, and knew him pretty well, and so I was delighted to have this in our Chemical Fund portfolio and, if we can have that chart, we'll see what some of that experience was like.

When I joined the board and first looked at this, we had a modest holding. At the equivalent of $1.50 a share for the present stock, it was not one of our largest portfolio positions. Our chairman, Bert Eberstadt, was a great believer, and then I told him what was always the Murray rule. Ask the question, what do you do on a rights offering by a company? The Murray rule says you always exercise your rights, and then you go out and buy an equivalent amount more. Always exercise your rights. Always buy more at the time when the stock is under pressure from the rights offering. So when I came to disclose that Murray's rule to Bert Eberstadt, I found that I needn't. He had already adopted the Eberstadt rule, which was identical. So off we went by exercising our rights in this sequence of financing.

Everything came through in great style. We all know about the development of the Xerox copier, and we had an absolutely unique problem. Our problem was the fund prospectus says no more than 5 percent in any company and, what do you know, our Xerox holding was in excess of 10 percent of the portfolio. We couldn't buy anymore obviously after we had reached 5 percent but we didn't have to sell.

But we were coming up to that period of time when you ask the question, that old question. Can that rate of growth in the enterprise continue indefinitely? And, clearly, we would be starving to death very soon because all of our resources would be applied to the manufacturer and use of copiers.

So sometimes we said, What about that familiar phenomenon of the S-curve[7] in the life of an industry, in the life of a company? You have that start-up period. You get going and then you go through that period of the most rapid growth, and then it kind of turns down. The rate of change declines and then maybe, sometime, you'll actually come to a mature phase, and, at that part of the S-curve, this is beginning to roll over. All kinds of things could happen. You could go through one S-curve, and you could start another. There's nothing so inevitable about that widely observed phenomenon of the life cycle of a company or an industry that says it is preordained.

Well, it's one of the things you have to think about, and we go along here, and the company makes a few acquisitions and, at this juncture, here they turn around and buy a computer company, Scientific Data Systems, and we sat around and we said uh-huh, that's it. One of the most frequently observable signs of the maturing of an industry, a product, or a company is when the management, sitting down, looking into the future, says we ought to diversify. We ought to broaden our product line. We ought to do all of those things which leads us cynical security analysts to say this company is moving its resources and its efforts away from what it knows how to do best and it almost, by definition, the new undertakings of what they do not know how to manage and develop as effectively. Well, you could say, this is reasonably related in some way to the copying business, and it is not too far removed, but we decided that we had had a wonderful experience with the Xerox Corporation. We had owned it during the period of accelerating growth, and, at these price levels, we did not want to be a continuing part owner on the same scale. So we liquidated through this period here and went elsewhere.

As spectators, of course, we watched and when the time came, when they organized Xerox Financial Services entering that plus competitive business called "Property and Casualty Insurance" and related aspects of financial management, mutual funds, and the whole array, we could always say, this is not the company that this was. This is the most important, single, fundamental analytical problem that we have to face. Where do you stand in the life cycle? is question number one.

Question number two: What steps are being taken in the allocation of resources, and we are talking about all kinds of resources, not just what we read in the financial statements, what we can get our hands on? But what about managerial resources, key staff decision makers, and the time and the effort being expended on the different areas of activity? This is a tough problem for us outsiders. We don't have a chance to sit in the boardroom and listen while people are going through the process of making those decisions, but it is the most important thing about our valuation of the company and its prospects.

Let's turn now to another kind of a company. By chance, it happens that this has been a widely discussed enterprise. It's Westinghouse Electric. Very different characteristics of where it stands in the life cycle, where it stands on that S-curve. We're well past the early start-up period in their lines of business, and we're talking about what we ordinarily speak of as a mature company, long established in central station electric power and a lot of different related lines of activity in what we generally speak of as electrical equipment. If I can have that chart, we'll see something of the recent past history, although we know that this is a much older company than what is reflected on our chart.

Now we're not looking at an emerging new technology. We're looking at some pretty well-established lines of business. We're looking at relatively developed marketplaces, and we're addressing the process that a company goes through when it reaches that period of maturity, and it looks down the road and says, I've got a pretty good growing stream of earning power in place. I'm able to increase my dividends quite regularly in a significant way, but as I look down the road, it's not just that I've got a real tough competitor out there called General Electric in most of my lines of activity, but I really can't see ahead of me the kinds of product development in the good old electrical equipment business. What do I do? I broaden out my product line to identify other alternative areas.

What do you know, I buy an office furniture company. The precise relationship, a potential synergy of office furniture and electrical equipment, may not be crystal clear to any of us but maybe our imagination is limited.

How about going further, integrating forward as well as backward in the electrical equipment industry. Okay, follow your customers for your central station equipment with all of the controlled systems and the other features. Now, since a lot of what we do is kind of electrical, it makes sense, doesn't it, to own a radio network. Westinghouse Radio System, quite successful, quite a good profitable growing line of activity. Again, the synergy isn't precisely clear to any of us.

But let's stay right with our basic business if you're selling appliances. Of course, you want to have a captive finance company to facilitate installment sales by your dealers of white goods.[8] Okay, so we have Westinghouse Credit but really, we all know that the installments sales business isn't of real exciting growth, high profitable area of finance. So what we ought to do with the credit company is broaden the scale of its activities now that we have become knowledgeable and expert in financial markets. So let's go ahead now, and if we look over our shoulder and see what our General Electric Credit and General Electric Capital have done, we realize that the range and opportunities are virtually unlimited. Off we go.

Don't need to stop at financing of new ventures and new companies. There's a wonderful wave of opportunity in real estate finance as we get into the 1980s, and it's a spectacular boom. One of the things most of us have learned is that it's much better to be an early starter in a broad line of activity than to be a latecomer. One of the best opportunities you are going to have in real estate investment after this boom has been rolling for some years. You have an excellent opportunity to acquire the opportunities which others had passed by.

The knowledgeable people in this business, if they were really knowledgeable, don't you think they did the best deals in the whole business of the financing of shopping centers? Don't you have to presume that the best-located shopping centers are the ones that were built first? That people know what they are doing through an analytical process? The twenty-seventh shopping center is not in the same class with the seventh shopping center of one of the major chains.

So what happens if you enter into this kind of diversifying in areas where you carry into, you bring with you into that activity no special edge, no special skill or insight as to the potential. So you ask yourself, as an analyst, here as a spectator, you say to yourself, I wonder what goes on in the Westinghouse boardroom. I'd really like to know how these decisions are reached.

On this subject, I learned from a very interesting instructor. You all know him. His name is Louis Gilbert, one of the most famous annual meeting hecklers and troublemakers known to man. I talked to him. One of my jobs when I was at the bank was that the chairman had me visit with Mr. Gilbert before the annual meeting and we could settle on the ground rules.

You ask any question you want within these bounds, and we are not going to disclose information that would be damaging to the company but beyond that, feel free, we'll be ready. Have you got any hints you'd like to give me on what areas you might cover? And sure, I get some hints, and we sit down and be prepared and, as you remember, he always started with banks, and so we had a chance to have a front row seat. And I used to say to Lou, "Gee, you know some of the things you talk about are really not that critical in the way of determining the future of the company." And his answer, I learned from him was, "Look there is never a time when they're going to invite me into the boardroom for those decisions. How can I get an insight on how this company goes about making decisions?" And he said, "Gee, I know how." I can see how they react to one of these kinds of questions where I have found a way to touch a sensitive nerve and the way they deal with those kinds of questions that you say are not very important is illustrative of how the mind works.

Well years ago, I kind of applied this technique in looking at Westinghouse. What information did I have about Westinghouse? I had information on how they made their strategic decisions about their pension fund. I had an opportunity of talking with the in-house staff that was acting on behalf of Westinghouse as planned sponsor to see what instructions those people were given, and they were not their thoughts necessarily and there was, in fact, a turn-over in that staff.

But what Westinghouse was giving its managers was what I would call a liquidity requirement. You have to design your asset mix significantly to reduce the exposure to a negative return of any size. Think about that. Think about its implications for the long-term total return of that asset for which, in a fundamental sense, there was not a liquidity requirement. It was truly a classic case long-term, long-time horizon pension fund investment where you're in one of the best places known to man for putting up with the illiquidity of owning variable assets, and as I learned, and I could see how Westinghouse was addressing that problem and there seemed to be a thought-out policy conclusion. Is that the way they make their critical decisions? It might not be, but it was a significant indicator.

I had one experience where I really did have a look. Some years ago, you may remember when United Technology made a bid for Babcock and Wilcox on a hostile takeover on practically no notice at all. Counsels for Babcock and Wilcox recruited me to assist in defending Babcock and Wilcox from this takeover. Because this was now in the courtroom, and you had rights of discovery. I had a chance to hold in my hand precisely the memorandum that was distributed to the board of directors of United Technology on the day when the chairman came in and said, "I recommend that we make a bid of X hundred million dollars for Babcock and Wilcox, and here is your backup material." And I went through that backup material, and I said to myself, "If Mario Gabelli had turned in that as a paper to me in my security analysis class, I know exactly what I would have done with it. Mario, will you go back and start over and give me some real substantive analysis of Babcock and Wilcox. I can't possibly make a decision even to buy an odd lot on the basis of this presentation, no less make a bid, multibillion of dollars of a bid, to acquire it."

It appeared from the material that the chairman came in and said we'd been thinking about our future. We'd been thinking about diversification. Now that we have Carrier and we have Otis Elevator, we really ought to have Babcock and Wilcox. And this is a right price that we're going to get it. As far as anybody knows, nobody sitting around the table said, "Oh no, just a darn minute, you haven't established a thesis for that kind of a major decision. Let's have a real session. Don't hand me a worn copy of *Moody's Industrial Manual*[9] and expect me to make that kind of a decision." Well, that's not the way they operated, but I did get some real insight into how critical major decisions were made in that case, in that company. Now, when we really get into our problems of valuation, what we really get into is the problem of trying to appraise the future of the enterprise, and we'd done all of our financial statement analysis. We have put together the best picture of quantitative information, still haven't finished the task.

Some of the qualitative factors, some of the decision-making processes, will, of course, show up in the corporate history because that is indeed what they did, but what we really want to know is, given our present picture, the best picture we can put together of the earning power of the enterprise. What resource have we in terms of the managerial decision-making process that will give us confidence that when that totally new situation emerges and, my past history is quite irrelevant, what is the best course of action in that new and different environment—how are they going to react? What will be the analytical process? What factors will they weigh in reaching those decisions? In this respect, we have only some not very good techniques to measure the prospects of getting good decisions. One of the things we can do, however, is to get some sense of what the underlying trends are for this line of business and for this company.

One time, in talking with Ben Graham about stock valuation, he said to me, and I always remembered this so distinctively, he said, "Tell me about the earning power of a company and I'll do the valuation on the back of an envelope." You can see this is what we were really talking about last time when we said that the valuation is simple. It's D over K minus G. All we need to know is the earning power, the characteristics of the earning power, its stability, predictability, those kinds of characteristics and its growth.

Murray is referring to the Gordon growth model, the formula for which is:

$$P = D/(K - G)$$

where D equals the dividend, K equals the discount rate, and G equals the long-term growth rate. Using the formula, value equals the annual dividend (D) divided by the difference between the discount rate (K) and the long-term growth rate (G). The formula is extremely sensitive to the choice of long-term growth rate, which makes it hard to use when valuing companies.

What Graham and Dodd is saying, "Remember, growth is not a quantitative factor. Growth is a qualitative factor." And every time I say that to anybody, I see that skepticism. What do you mean, growth is not a quantitative factor? When I talk about growth, when I discuss growth, I'm always talking about a quantitative number. I am anticipating a growth of, we did it on the screen, it was 6½ percent for equities taken as a whole. What do you mean it isn't quantitative? I mean exactly that. What we are talking about is the characteristics of a stream of earning power. We're talking about characteristics, consistency, predictability, the level of the earning stream, the tendency for it to stabilize or even decline.

We're talking about where are you on that S-curve in terms of the life cycle of an industry, of the economic development and maturing of a line of business or a corporate enterprise. So what we're saying is, I really want to know, as best I can figure it out, where I am in relation to the economic and capital markets, in competitive environments as I look ahead out there in my seven-year framing of expectations, and I will focus, as we said, on about the midpoint or the fourth year.

Let me look then at, by quantitative measures that I have used, I measured the level of profitability and the rate of change over a reasonably comprehensive period of time like a business cycle or its equivalent in this particular industry. When I look at that earning power, the first thing I ask is, "Where did it come from?"

The finest asset resource of a security analyst is one simple ratio, capital turnover, the way I've always expressed this. Capital turnover is the analyst's best friend. And we all know, as analysts, we need friends in the worst way. Try it sometime. Look at the capital turnover ratio of a company over an extended period of time. Extraordinary stability is one of the characteristics that you will observe in many instances. Remember now, I'm talking about the best estimate I can put together and not what that nifty financial officer has passed out, but the best measure I can get of earnings that I got some notion about whether they are clean, clear, and expressive.

Capital, total capital. I'm talking about everything that's on the balance sheet and all of the things that aren't on the balance sheet. I'm going to capitalize the leases, and I'm going to put in all of the elements of debt, long-term, short-term, all of the elements of equity, and when I divide that into my sales figure, I've got a capital turnover ratio. The reason why this is such a wonderful friend for the analyst is you will find this is extraordinarily stable unless there is a change in the nature of the company's business. That is exactly what you're looking for.

Tell me now, can I look back over some history and say, that's a good guide or that's illustrative of this company's past earning power, or do I have to say to myself, "Now, wait a minute, wait a minute, there is a discontinuity in that pattern. There is a change of life"? Maybe, I'm getting up to that mature point on the S-curve. Maybe, instead of concentrating on electrical equipment, I'm concentrating on office furniture or any of those other kinds of activities. My picture of leading copiers through time was a picture in which there were not financial services, property and casualty insurance component, and that's going to show up. Sure enough, my capital turnover ratio was going to start to change. So you can say, with a good deal of conviction, that something has happened. Something has happened to the company, or maybe something has happened to the manner in which it was capitalized.

We have talked all the way through here about valuing a company. We haven't said a word about capital structure. We treated that as not a significant factor at all. If we are valuing the company, that's absolutely correct that we should pay no attention to how it's capitalized. Let us identify the value of the enterprise, and then we can turn to how the productivity of the enterprise is distributed among different holders of securities, and finally we can get down to the question of the share of equity.

Now, here we get right back to a couple of Nobel Prize–winning financial types by the name of Modigliani and Miller.[10] Modigliani and Miller gave us all some good fresh thinking when they said that the cost of capital for a company is independent of the mix between debt and equity. It doesn't matter how you capitalize the company. The effects will be authentic. There are benefits to debt financing for the equity, but the equity return will be more variable as you introduce leverage.

AUTHORS' NOTE

Franco Modigliani and Merton Miller published a paper in 1958 contending that, in a perfectly efficient market, the capital structure that a corporation uses is irrelevant to its overall value. In other words, changing the capital structure will not change the company's valuation. Two key assumptions in their proposition are that the stock price is efficiently set and that there are no tax benefits from issuing debt. The two assumptions do not hold in the real world, and several research studies have been published since 1958 that refute the original Modigliani and Miller proposition.

All very interesting and well thought out and clear, except that the other academics said, "Just a minute, gentlemen, you are not taking account of the fact that there's a tax subsidy to debt that does not apply to equity because we have a thing that we call a corporate income tax." It's really not a corporate income tax, I submit. It's an excise tax levied on consumers, and there's no significant evidence that, in fact, the corporate income tax comes to rest on corporate profits. Don't let that word get outside this room. I'm still happy that the Congressman enjoyed the illusion that they are taxing corporate profits and, somehow or other, they never look at the long history of corporate profitability when we reduce the corporate income tax from 90 percent in wartime down to 50, to 40, to wherever. What do you know? Corporate profits don't go through the roof. Corporate profits are the real mainsprings of economic growth and development, and they are what feed the incentives for making new investments, and it's always the after-tax return on the equity that matters.

In any event, to the extent that you use debt, forgetting now the leverage factor related to that bond contract which we speak of in our friendly way as of a contract that assures that the lender will be the loser and the borrower would be the winner, if there is any inflation at work in a society, entirely apart from that, what we're saying is on this part of your earnings represented by your use of debt, you don't have to earn, in the marketplace, that excise tax which you have to pay to the Internal Revenue Service because they have an item called a corporate income tax. So it's clear: you have to earn less, your cost of capital is lower, if you make use of debt. You could think of the dash line as Modigliani and Miller. You could think of my rough curve here as Graham and Dodd.

In the earlier editions, they always had a section called, "In Defense of Debt." They were talking about, "You'll enhance the value of the enterprise; you'll reduce the cost of capital by the judicious use of debt." How much debt? Well, use a round number. American industry, I'm excluding now finance companies, or financial institutions, or public utilities and industrial, broadly speaking, somewhere around one-third maximizes value and return to equity.

What happens out here that this cost goes through the roof? What do you get up here, anywhere near 70 percent debt and 30 percent equity? Answer: We're talking about something entirely different. We're not talking about the fact that leverage magnifies the variability of reported earnings. If we don't care about liquidity, we couldn't care less as long as you have raised the average total return of the enterprise. But what is your capacity to stay through periods of adversity? Have you a margin of safety so that I do not need to worry about an insolvency risk at some point, and if I get out here for industrial companies and I'm coming out towards two-thirds debt or more? In a great many instances, that loss of creditworthiness, that exposure to insolvency risk, has become very real.

Okay, what does this tell us about equity valuation? It tells us a great deal. It provides us clear thinking on this, provides us with exceptional investment opportunities. Would you believe that equity analysts are at work every day in the financial community doing earnings projections? Turn the page quickly on the balance sheet, never even ask themselves or those guys down the hall who work on bonds about creditworthiness.

Do you have an exposure by reason of the high financial leverage to insolvency? I grew up in the days when we used to debate whether it was ever conceivable that an airline could go bankrupt. The consensus was that an airline couldn't. After all, we had regulatory support, all that kind of stuff. In due course, of course, we learned, What was the airline problem? What has it been? How can major worldwide airlines go completely down the drain? Answer: This is a business with very high operating leverage. If you got high operating leverage, and you put on top of that very high financial leverage, what is the exposure to serious disappointment in your investment experience? The answer is that it's very, very great. It's very difficult, as we study such matters, to set a high enough rate on our old friend, capital K, the rate of return demanded in the valuation of that enterprise.

We don't have, you know, we're pretty good at measuring risk and expected returns when we're somewhere in the middle ground of corporate finance and corporate activity. But at the extremes, we really have great difficulty in equating the exposure to permanent capital loss and the return that we anticipate. This is the old junk bond question.

Years ago, I was on the committee for the "National Bureau Study of Corporate Bonds, 1900 to 1944," Brad Hitman's analysis, the most complete that has ever been made, and you took corporate bonds of all kinds and in sizes from the turn of the century through 1944, and you looked at the experience. What did you find? You found that, after allowance for default loss, you got a higher realized return on the lower quality issues. Fascinating, and you go through the process, you go through the analysis, and say, "Yeah, yeah, I could see how that could be."

There are a lot of investors who can't stand the illiquidity. They can't stand the price variability of lower quality issues and, in point of fact, we have a regulatory system for financial institutions that makes absolutely certain that you will be required to liquidate such assets at the lowest, nearly the lowest possible prices. So, gee, that's an unforeseen investment opportunity. Don't buy double A and triple A bonds. After all, they could only go down in their level of perceived creditworthiness.

Get in there on BA candidates[11] for the double A standards as we use them conventionally. Do your analysis. Select them. Pick up that additional return in the marketplace. Try to set it aside systematically as a reserve against the inevitability that not every one of your selections is going to be perfect and, if you do that, you get enough of a differential in yield to cover that loss reserve, you'll come out ahead.

Fine. My name happens to be, I got the same bald head, but I changed my name today to Milken. Now I want to tell you, you can see. Look at the study. It's all there. It's documented. You ought to buy the lower quality of securities and diversify your portfolio, and you'll come up with a superior reserve and an experience with your executive life insurance company.

Now, what went wrong? What's the misreading? The misreading is really very simple. You could talk about diversification, and you could talk about different economic sectors but there's another element of diversification. As soon as we sit down to think about it, there's something called diversification over time, diversification over time.

You'll buy junk bonds when they're the apple of everybody's eye, and you'll buy them when they haven't got a friend in the world, and those wonderful regulators are out there requiring you to liquidate those portions of your assets which is nothing to do, of course, with the inherent financial position of the individual borrowers. It's simply because they don't make the grade of one of the rating systems designed by regulators.

Well, the great investment opportunity of all time is to follow what happens in the regulatory process. But many of you remember the experience of 1928. In 1928, the students of the legal trust for bonds and saving banks[12] did a study. And they looked back over the previous history of the railroad industry, and they said, "We have set too high standards for legal railroad bonds." So they multiplied the eligible list by a factor of 2 to 2½ times. It went down through the quality ranks that far because, in the preceding decade or more, those bonds had been perfectly safe. Wonderful exercise, putting that large volume of railroad bonds on the eligibility list for legal trust and for savings banks.

The default rate in that particular addition to the list, if memory serves me, was somewhere in the neighborhood of 40 percent, and, of course, many that didn't actually default had their prices cut by half or two-thirds, and the regulatory authorities, now that these were removed from the legal list, would be insistent about the financial institution liquidating those securities. I don't want to make you feel badly because you all missed it. The greatest investment opportunity of this century was the opportunity to buy those defaulted railroad bonds.

The Wabash five and a halves[13] of 1975 that I bought at 7½ were paid off in full with back interest on the merger with the Pennsylvania Railroad.[14] The kinds of things we all dream about and say, "Gee, you suppose it might happen again sometime." Pretty good case, pretty good case, now for looking through the wreckage of the junk bond period to identify grossly undervalued securities placed in that position by those wonderful public servants called the staff of regulatory bodies.

It's not a question of, Have you ever analyzed a security? It's a question of whether you have read and understand that "big book,"[15] and the big book tells you what the rules are for the FDIC or for any one of the regulatory bodies of what is an acceptable investment. We should always add, in hindsight; that is, don't ask me about what may happen in the future.

What we come back to, it seems to me, is the necessity of integrating the analytical process. When we set that capital K and we tried to take account of our exposure to disappointment, as contrasted with owning an index fund, let's say, and taking whatever comes in the way of returns to equities, how do we adequately come to a conclusion about what we should demand in this case? What we'd like to do is assemble a high expected return of security, recognizing that since we are not infallible, we will own several and we will achieve the disappointment-reducing process of diversifying across different areas of economic activities.

Different kinds of industries and companies whose resolution of whatever problems lie ahead will be found from different approaches and techniques. Through all of this, we have to take account of those qualitative factors, qualitative factors.

I've talked a lot about the management factor and a very good lesson that we learned is brought right from the bridge table. Don't count the same trick twice. Don't pay a high price for that security because it's profitable, it's consistent, it's an industry leader. We do all of that in our calculation of what the earning power is, and let's say that the picture is excellent. We think that the earning power prospects are really quite outstanding for this company. Okay, crank that right into your calculation of normal earning power, but when you come to capitalize that in setting your intrinsic value, don't come back and say, "Gee, this is a company with very strong underpinnings, so I ought to apply a higher multiple to that expected earnings stream because it's so good." That is what we call counting the same trick twice.

Murray raises an important insight with his comments. By definition, earning power is an estimate of what a company can earn under "normal" conditions and should represent sustainable future earnings. If the earning power is estimated correctly, there should be no reason to increase the discount rate or lower the multiple used to value those earnings.

Your estimation of normal earning power for this enterprise is already reflecting all of the favorable features and strengths of the enterprise. Don't go now and say this is a fine company; I ought to be willing to pay an additional premium to own it. You've already taken account of those positive favorable expectations.

Turn this upside down. Talk about the company that's in the doldrums and has all kinds of problems and doesn't seem to be getting anywhere. You have made, therefore, a pretty darn cynical estimate of what that normal earning power is like. You say, "I'm not looking for great growth and increasing levels of profitability. I don't expect that my capital turnover ratio is going to start marching back magnificently uphill and lead to really a new era of profitability for this company."

We've gone through that whole exercise. Then don't say I ought to capitalize this very moderate set of expectations about the company's future at a very low multiple. And this is the same exercise we go through with cyclical companies, isn't it?

Somebody says, "Oh, you can't buy that company. Don't you realize it's selling at thirty-seven times last year's earnings." And you will say, "Well, thanks, I could read that in that little column in my daily newspaper and you haven't told me anything about the earning power of this enterprise if we were not still in the throes of this fairly protracted and major recession that hit especially hard this line of business under these circumstances."

So the name of the game is to keep clear and distinct the difference between reported earnings and the earning power of an enterprise, the difference between temporary short-term and long-term fundamental factors affecting a company. It's asking a lot that we should turn around and be hard-nosed, unemotional, tightly disciplined analysts and decision makers.

No, we don't have to be that good. We don't have to be that rigorous. We got a world full of people setting prices on securities who are doing it emotionally, illogically, without an understanding of the enterprise that they are thinking about buying or selling.

And we've got on our side, if we are willing to work at it, we've got two characteristics on the rest of the world out there. One is they're lazy. Most people are lazy deep down in their hearts but we're talking about a line of business. There are no returns to laziness. There are lots of returns to good old-fashioned hard work.

What's the second advantage we have? If we practice it, we can exercise something called patience, which, as I said before, is in terribly short supply everywhere. And certainly, in this business where we value, we try to appraise the value of a long-term investment experience in time dimensions like a quarter.

One of the great triumphs of my career was persuading an investment committee for a pension fund that they would accept our rule. They would never see any performance calculation that covered a period of less than three years. It was tough, I want to tell you and, over all the years, they always tried to break this down. We know, Roger, we only look at three years. However, in that last market experience, how did we do then? And my answer was, "Don't worry about that. I'll watch that for you and if it suggests anything of significance, you'll hear from me." Otherwise, our measurement period is three years. It's always three years. We'll move it forward each quarter and you'll realize, of course, they were only taking interim snapshots because we sat together and we've looked at your actuarial reports, and we know that your time horizon as a relatively mature company is only somewhat shorter but it's fifty years.

Let us not judge how effectively we have solved an investment management problem in a fifteen-year time dimension by an observation of what happened in the last three months. It took a long time, but we finally got them to accept that proposition because they learned, if they didn't accept it, so help me, they had to suffer through a lecture, as you have suffered so nicely this morning.

Thanks a lot.

13

LECTURE 4—CONVERGENCE OF PRICE AND VALUE

(February 12, 1993)

DOUG JAMIESON:[1] Hello, my name is Doug Jamieson. I am the chief operating officer of Gabelli Asset Management Company [GAMCO]. On behalf of the managing directors of GAMCO, it is my privilege to introduce to you a series of lectures given by Professor Roger F. Murray and sponsored by our firm.

In 1966, Mario Gabelli aced his course in security analysis at Columbia Business School. Roger Murray was Gabelli's professor who, as Ben Graham's successor, carried on the tradition of the Graham and Dodd approach to security analysis. The basic tenet of this approach is that the stock market's pricing of securities is often based on faulty and irrational analysis. The price of a security only occasionally coincides with its intrinsic value.

At GAMCO, we use the principles developed and taught by Ben Graham, David Dodd, and Roger Murray in performing the fundamental analysis employed in the management of our client accounts. Our object is to earn annual returns in excess of 10 percent of inflation. We have exceeded this target by compounding the assets entrusted to us at the rate of 20 percent annually since we founded our firm fifteen years ago.

Graham and Dodd's *Security Analysis* has been the definitive work in the investment field for over fifty years. It created the profession of financial analysis. In 1988, Roger Murray coauthored the completely updated and modernized fifth edition.

In addition to his writing and teaching career, Professor Murray has been an investment manager, a trustee, the founding director of the Investor Responsibility Research Center [IRRC], and the originator of the individual retirement account [IRA] concept. It is a distinct pleasure to introduce Professor Roger F. Murray. Thank you.

GABELLI: *Convergence* is a word that is used to denote a lot of things. Some of the media today are talking about interactivity, talking about the convergence of the computer, the cable, the television, cellular. But here in convergence, we are going to talk about price and value.

Gabelli Asset Management has been privileged to sponsor these lectures. All of you that have been attending should be aware there is a minor quiz and a small diploma if you pass it at the end, and I don't want the pressure to rise on such a wonderful day. But before Roger starts the lecture, on behalf of all the security analysts, past, present, and future, Roger, thank you. And for myself, it is a distinct privilege. For those of us that were blessed to listen to you at Columbia for those years that you were casting those insights into intrinsic valuation and insights into the value-added process, I also want to thank you again.

As you know, we are taping these lectures and putting them into the Roger Murray Library, which we are going to create at a place where—we still have to figure out where, Roger. In fact, when we buy a building, we may even call it the—we may even have a dedication ceremony, and the way I make decisions, it may take about five or ten more years, so, we will have you there for the dedication of it. We will put in that library anything to do with Graham and Dodd, including these tapes. So we hope that this is the beginning of a continuing twenty-year lecture series.

Roger, I am turning the podium and classroom over to you.
MURRAY: In some respects, we are addressing this morning the most difficult aspect of our undertaking. The one thing we all know

is that returns, realized returns, and investment experience are very much a function of time. So we always are examining in some respect the time value of an idea, and when we think about the potential convergence of price on intrinsic value, the first question we have to ask ourselves, because it is so determinative of the measurable outcome is, How soon? What can we do in the way of anticipating or predicting how long it will take for that intrinsic value acting as a magnet on price to bring about what we think of as a logical, rational, economic result?

One of the interesting dimensions of this whole question is, of course, the different phases in the market for equity securities. We now have some pretty good measures. How do value stocks perform relative to growth stocks? And we know that from 1973 to 1981, that is an eight-year span, value performed better than growth in security markets. We can look back to the next span, '81 to '85—standoff: not much difference in the behavior of growth versus value. Comes 1985 to 1990, growth outperformed value. We had a standoff in 1991. In 1992, both did well. And, of course, as we think about this today, our big question is, What's next? What do we see as the likely leaders for the next span of time?

Fascinating experience with what are called small cap, medium-sized capitalization companies. In June 1983, that wonderful market in small caps that had been so fabulously profitable stopped, and it is fair to say that from June '83 to October 1990, there was, indeed, a kind of a private bear market in small caps when they underperformed large caps, not by any trivial amount, but by something like 45 percent in relative performance.

Now the interesting thing is that we are looking at some fairly extended periods of time, and so, as the small cap market has emerged and performed well, people say, "This isn't any kind of a short-term development." Just think, it was seven or eight years on the last negative period for small caps, and we can look forward to a long, extended period of time in which small caps will outperform large cap stocks. Very interesting and very appealing, as many have changed their portfolio mix to include a larger component of small and midcap stocks. Interesting question, of course, is whether any of those historical time periods have any relevance whatever to the future. But I think if we think about that for just a short while, we will say there is nothing; the calendar won't help us.

The important determinant of whether one sector, whether it be growth versus value or small cap versus midcap versus large cap, has got to be a function of some price relationships, and the calendar, you could say, is almost irrelevant. If the relationship of market prices to some expectations about intrinsic value, the disparity between the two, as we have talked about it, has been pictured as a magnet: a drawing together of market prices towards some notion of an underlying value which has some real substance to it.

There is, however, one thing that most of us have concluded from observation. A very simple notion when we look at price behavior. What we observe is that major changes tend to be rounded rather than sharp points. What I mean by that is an advancing price of many kinds of commodities and financial assets tends to be rounded rather than an abrupt reversal, which is to say that one of the characteristics of a major top or bottom in prices is that period in which the rate of change diminishes, and that is what gives us, obviously, rounded rather than sharp changes in prices.

Some years ago, like forty or thereabouts, a man who had no experience in securities markets whatever came and talked with some of us about that phenomenon, and he showed us some very interesting charts which he had constructed for freely moving commodity prices. What he said to us was, "If you look at a smoothing of those price records, you will see that the diminishing rate of return change was a reliable forecaster of a change in direction." After working with commodities for a number of years, he was encouraged to apply his techniques to stock prices. His name was Doug Hanna. I don't know that he has ever been famous for these exercises of his, but we see them all the time used as a measure in equity markets of relative strength.

The proposition is that if you want to get some sense of when there will be an acceleration in the relative price movement of a security or an industry in which you are interested, take a look at how investors are voting. Are they expressing a preference for the subject company or the subject industry, as contrasted with their attitude toward all equities? And if you measure the price change of a particular industry or company, always as a relative . . . relative to the market taken as a whole, you will see an expression of preferences which people are expressing in their actual decisions to prefer one company or one industry to another.

So let's look at this first chart and where we can take a look at an expression of those preferences by investors. What I have used here is the drug industry, which is a very interesting case. Here is an industry with a very stable progress of earnings, consistent growth at a high rate. This you will observe of the major pharmaceutical companies. We haven't got biotech in here to any significant extent. We had a little shortfall of two or three of the major companies in that interval. Pfizer and Upjohn were the laggards, but the general trend of earning power exhibited in this long-term chart was really quite continuous.

Now, the bottom line here is the relative strength. How did this industry composite compare with the S&P 500 across this period of time? You see that long span where the industry was well liked in proportion to its size as a component, but then comes the latter period here where we have that spectacular period of relative strength. What was that saying to investment decision makers? It was saying, in effect, if you were thinking about applying some research time to the drug industry, if you were thinking about including a larger proportion of pharmaceutical companies in your portfolio, you had better not linger. In a sense, you could say that whatever your decision was, remember there were other people out there who were expressing a strong preference for this industry, and if you expected to be an advantageous buyer of companies in this industry, you had better get down to business. If you had a long list of ideas that you wanted to pursue, you would say to yourself, "I don't have a great deal of time to go off and study this one because people out there are eagerly expressing a preference for that industry."

Of course, it is also fascinating to see how that year-end 1991 explosion in quality growth pricing, very inclusive of drugs, of course, took relative strength up into a brand-new area. And if you look at the numerical expression here on the side, you would say to yourself, "Gosh, on a relative strength basis, this was on the order of a 50 percent increase in the expression of preference for this industry."

Really now on the fundamentals of the industry, was there a change of that dimension in its prospects, or are we looking at one of those phenomena that we see, particularly at the ends of reporting periods? If the drugs have done well, if I am going to show my portfolio to my clients or my investors, I surely ought to have a strong representation of that industry which has been doing well. That kind of portfolio fixing and adjusting at the end of reporting periods is an unfortunate kind of phenomenon that takes place, and one about which one should be very, very thoughtful and analytical.

The other striking phenomena that you see there is that relative strength told you about forces in motion, and preferences being expressed in the marketplace never told you anything about the turning point, which is to say that, at the end of 1991, relative strength was telling you, go right ahead. Trees really grow to the sky. You don't have to think about concepts like intrinsic value or economic value. Everybody is seeing the future through rose-colored glasses, and there is no end in sight.

In other words, what we are getting here is not a change in the underlying characteristics of an industry; this is all in the nature of a change in people's expectations about the future. Investing in expectations—and people's sentiment, and sometimes irrational preferences—is a very risky and uncertain business. Something about which it is well to remind ourselves that, as financial analysts, we really are not very well qualified to make forecasts about what people will be thinking, what they will be imagining, and what kinds of preferences they will express.

Let's turn now to a different example, and we will look at Deere & Company, a major cyclical company, a very interesting enterprise. We are looking now at the economics of agriculture and farm equipment. We are looking at earth-moving equipment. We can think in terms these days about infrastructure, and we can even come out on Saturday afternoons and push a John Deere lawn mower at home. On this kind of a busy chart, it is not too easy to watch the relative strength line, but there it is—moving up and down quite dramatically. An interesting feature of that chart is it has no lead or lag visible. If you look at when was relative strength greatest— answer, right at the peak. When was it lowest? Right at the bottom. And the conformity of those lines of relative strength and price behavior is very, very close.

What might one conclude from this? It seems to me you conclude that I can't get any strength . . . any help from relative strength if I am looking at a company like this. In fact, in many respects, this is my case, where I must operate entirely on my own. If I am going to be a buyer at the trough—and you can think of this as relative performance—if I am going to be a buyer at the trough and not be a buyer at the peak, I am strictly on my own. I may actually find a contrarian's role as my best stance in dealing with this kind of a cyclical enterprise, and to be a successful investor in Deere, obviously not like the drug industry, is it? This is really a cyclical kind of an undertaking. This is where the payoff from fundamental analytical value can be at its highest because here is where we are afforded an opportunity to reach some useful conclusions about earning power across cycles of this particular company in this particular industry.

If we have some concepts in which we have confidence about the intrinsic value of Deere and Company, we have some of the kind of equipment that we need to make thoughtful analytical judgments about when we want to be in the company and when we are happy to pass.

One thought that emerges from looking at this kind of a chart, where we think about the preferences expressed by other people: this is an old technician's notion about overhead supply. We all joke and smile at some of the formations the technicians identify, like good old heads and shoulders, and all kinds of breakout points, and all kinds of things like that fundamentally we recognize as without any real underlying validity. And yet we know that there is a phenomenon that curiously influences decisions. If I had bought Deere up there near the top, and I have watched it decline, and finally it comes back to my cost price, I turn around and sell it. This is that magnificent formula for investment decision making called even-and-out. I have said to myself all through the decline, "If that stock ever gets back to what I paid for it, I will sell it." The rationale has to be that the management of Deere and Company, having realized what I paid for my shares, has decided to relax and let the business deteriorate now that they have brought me back to even. Unless, of course, there is some impact on the company's efforts from getting me back to even.

My accounting records for ownership really are not very material to my judgment on that particular investment. But this is a real phenomenon. It is not just a few silly individuals. There are all kinds of institutional portfolios, we have all seen it, where the manager was a little reluctant to show that significant realized loss. But once it has turned from red to black ink, the manager is quite happy to eliminate that from the portfolio.

Is this the way we ought to make our decisions? Heaven help us, no. But in framing our guesses about what price reaction may be and how it may be affected by historical prices, we really kind of need to recognize that even-and-out phenomena prevail in many, many situations. If, however, that previous peak is long enough ago, obviously that scientific investment method of taking losses for tax purposes will have diminished the impact.

Now I want to turn to a different case, another case that is very much in the news these days. It is the story of American Express. We have a long span of time here in which investors were expressing a negative preference, we might say, for American Express. What is interesting to me about this chart is this particular period in here, the year 1992. Now, 1992 was no different. The long saga of misadventures in American Express was not finished here in 1991. It continued with very few interruptions throughout last year. Interesting, interesting.

One interpretation of this could be that investors say, I know all the facts, and I followed all of the developments in American

Express. One conclusion is that they have done so many things wrong, there aren't any more that they could possibly do. Another, more constructive interpretation is you say, Really, the company is going through a whole set of different kinds of mishaps and misadventures but has still got a basic franchise that even this kind of a history will not fully destroy. So I am not going to be following each misstep along the way. At some point, I will come to the conclusion that there are enough basics in the picture and, in due course, something will happen. That judgment, incidentally, seems to have turned out to be a pretty good judgment. In point of fact, the signs of change in the boardroom have been dramatic, and for the first time, we might say, responsive to the underlying strategic, managerial, resource allocation challenges of the company.

So if you were going through the process of making a fundamental analysis of American Express in the last twelve or fifteen months, and you saw that there had been no further deterioration in investor attitudes and preferences and expectations about American Express, you could quite reasonably have said, "I am going to move that up on my agenda for a decision making from the bottom of the list up to the middle or, perhaps, well into the upper fraction of that listing of situations deserving of careful analytical investigation and consideration for serious investment."

Well, how far does one want to go with this kind of an external expression of opinions? Answer—not too far, not too far. One of the things that Doug Hanna demonstrated to us when he was introducing his relative strength concept was it can easily be misused, and you can react much too frequently. His advice, which I have followed with great benefit, is don't think about making judgments on the basis of a three-month or maybe even a six-month expression of preferences. There are too many random fluctuations, too much instability in this to make it at all reliable. Only use it where you can see a continuous and clear expression.

One of the things that I did do at the time was chart relative strength in three colors. Relative strength was plotted in red when the market trend was distinctly downward. It was plotted in green when the market trend was distinctly positive, and it came out in simple slate gray when there was no significant change. I always remember one of my favorite charts. I had one done on American Telephone, the old company. When did it show a positive trend? Always in red. When the market was doing poorly, good old Ma Bell was doing relatively well. I used it for the other extreme, what looks like great foresight, I must say, these days—I used Chrysler, and it was a disaster when the plotting was in red, and it was just great when the plotting was green.

This is a very simple and yet very interesting and useful kind of an exercise. It tells you what happens to people's preferences in different environments. And so if you are trying to structure a portfolio, and you would like to increase its defensive characteristics, it is worth a look at performance in the periods of general market optimism and pessimism. That is telling you something that you have also presumably verified from your underlying financial analysis, which is the consistency, reliability, predictability, characteristics of that earning power, that earning stream.

Well, none of these market perceptions or observations is really very reliable and, as we have observed, they will almost never give you reliable leads on turning points. But we are not stuck simply with those price observations. Nowadays, we can get IBES [Institutional Brokers Estimate System] reports where we can tell how many analysts are following a company—a very interesting statistic all by itself—and we can see an array of their forecasts of per-share earnings.

This is really a very useful body of knowledge in several respects. A well-qualified manager of my acquaintance didn't have available the number of analysts sending in estimates. He used a technique called the file drawer technique. How many brokerage-house reports did he receive on an individual company? When that file drawer got full, his conclusion was almost everything about this company by now ought to be in the price. But if his file drawer was practically empty and the only reports were long backdated, he could say quite logically, nobody or hardly anybody is really paying attention to this company. This is a candidate for mispricing because we don't have people out there eagerly keeping others informed. So his rule was you buy when the file drawer is practically empty, and when that file drawer begins to get pretty full, it is time to give some careful thought to unwinding that position.

AUTHORS' NOTE

Murray is referring to a neglect factor, which was a great source of potential investment opportunities in 1993. Unfortunately, neglected companies are significantly less prevalent these days because of the significant increase in the number of professional investors, all looking for mispriced and neglected stocks.

It seems like a kind of a silly way to make investment decisions, and yet there is an underlying logic to it. The only information that we might possess that has any value is what is not already expressed in the marketplace. There is enough efficiency in the marketplace to keep pulling those prices closer to intrinsic value if, and there is the big if, people are studying carefully and taking account of pieces of analytical work, which are rational and logical expressions of the underlying realities. But measures of what other people think we know must have very limited value. They can help us in doing one of the most difficult analytical tasks of all.

AUTHORS' NOTE

Murray is referring to two aspects of market efficiency—informational efficiency and analytical efficiency. If an investor possesses a piece of information the market does not have, that investor has an informational advantage. If an investor has a better estimate of value than the market, that investor has an analytical advantage. If the investor has neither an informational advantage nor an analytical advantage, then price equals value (for that investor), and there is no advantage or opportunity for excess returns.

You and I sit down, and we do a very thorough and complete and knowledgeable analysis of a company, and we come to the conclusion that, in this case, the market price is very closely in line with our best estimate of intrinsic value. What we have just learned is that our opinion, our judgment, our analysis is directly in line with the consensus of other knowledgeable people, and all we have done in our exercise is to satisfy ourselves that, indeed, the company is fairly valued. Having done all of that work and having confidence in the results, the most difficult task in the world is to take the work product and toss it into the circular file. It is our work. It is our investment. We ought to find something to do with it that is constructive. Very hard not to go back and say, "Gee, for all I know, I must have overlooked some very promising and positive aspects of this company that makes it undervalued."

What is influencing me is not the facts, not the underlying reality of the company. It is the impact of my personal investment in that company. The same problem that analysts have when they get to know a company really well. They get to know the people. They get to have a level of confidence in the information that they are receiving. They have all of those positives, which are all very interesting, but they may have no real material impact on the underlying intrinsic value of the company. We recognize that analysts are human beings, and what we have to do is not pretend that they aren't. We simply have to make allowance for these kinds of personal feelings, attitudes, and expectations.

AUTHORS' NOTE

When referring to analysts being human, Murray is acknowledging that all investors have innate biases. The field of behavioral finance has flourished since Murray's lectures in 1993. and the many biases that investors face are now better understood.

What we would like to do is find some good objective guides to help us in that baffling question: How long will it take for that convergence of price on value to occur? What we are looking for is . . . let's call them triggers, that say we have identified an undervalued company. Should we take our action now, or have we got lots of time in which we can continue our investigation and confirm our judgment?

AUTHORS' NOTE

Triggers are now referred to as catalysts. Catalysts come in two types—hard and soft. Hard catalysts are often specific events that can immediately change consensus expectations when disclosed.

Soft catalysts generally relate to the passage of time, with events unfolding that increase investor expectations, often because of the reduction in uncertainty relating to the company's financial performance as time passes.

Have we got some triggers? Well, I suppose, especially these days, we would all say, of course, changes in management are among the most important potential triggers. And we can all think of some good examples. Some of you will remember the day of Charlie Bluhdorn's[2] obituary in which the market price of Gulf & Western rose sharply and dramatically. We are all kind of glad that he was not there to see that happen because it is really pretty mortifying to think that his departure would be greeted with such resounding cheers.

For years, on the other hand, people sat around and looked at Occidental Petroleum, and they said, "You just wait. The day Armand Hammer[3] disappears, you are going to see that stock perform extraordinarily well." Hasn't happened, has it? I haven't looked lately, but the last time I looked, it was selling at a lower price. The answer was, under his long administration of Occidental Petroleum, he had created not some transitory kinds of problems that could be cured in the short run but that he had handed over a very major assignment, not only for restructuring the business lines but for restructuring the financial structure of the company.

There isn't a magic, then, in these kinds of management changes. Each one deserves some very careful analysis on its own. But in terms of drawing one's attention to the potential of an identified undervalued company, clearly this can be a real trigger.

Closely related and, in some respects, similar to changes in the executive suite are what we now refer to as restructurings. In this morning's paper, you could read, again, about the restructuring of Sears Roebuck's retailing and related activities. How many restructurings of Sears Roebuck have you read about? I must confess I have long since lost count. Sometimes they were addressing retailing. Sometimes they were addressing other parts of this diversified company.

It is not easy, for me at least, to put up the heat on the analysis of Sears Roebuck. It seems to me one is recognizing the reality that if this really is a problem easy to solve, it would have been solved long since, and that there are, indeed, major changes that will require a significant amount of time to place in effect. And we come away from that kind of an analysis saying to ourselves, The history of Sears Roebuck's profitability is not a reliable indicator of much of anything. It is perfectly clear, as we look at it now, that reported earnings, if properly deflated for the effects of inflation, have really not been the least bit impressive or satisfactory.

On the other hand, if we take a long look at the history of another widely diversified company called General Electric, we see how, in a long series of acquisitions and a long series of divestments, they have, indeed, restructured that company. Maybe everything hasn't been perfect. Maybe there have been some mistakes made. Maybe we don't know the full history of their ventures in the field of corporate finance and related lines, but at least they have taken us through fifteen or twenty years in which they were able to get out of some lines of activity of truly diminishing potential. And, indeed, frequently as we look at the many restructurings taking place under some very desirable shareholder expressions, frequently getting rid of, stripping off, ill-designed acquisitions over the years has been one of the most important contributors to success.

Now we have some other triggers that, of course, come to mind as being just key parts of the underlying analytical process: that's new products. And there is no area where this is any more significant than in an area like the drug business, where what is coming through that pipeline makes a huge difference in the level of earning power and the prospects for growth. When I started first investing in the drug business, when we didn't have the kind of information flow we have now, our strategy was to buy a package,[4] saying that pharmaceuticals were an excellent industry, strong growth prospects, all of those good features. But there was no way we, financial analysts, could identify a blockbuster new product and the potential effectiveness of research spending. Now, happily, we have so much better information, simple things like measurements of the numbers, all prescriptions of a new product through its start-up period gives us some insight.

There are also externalities that come into play, and it was interesting to see one here recently. We have those very serious storms, and you think of the extraordinary losses of many property and casualty companies. And if you are accurate in anticipating the outcome, you say, "I've got to buy the reinsurance companies like crazy." Logically, it makes good sense. If the reinsurance industry has the substantial participation in these kind of weather disasters, they will generate larger volume at higher premium rates and, across time, this will be constructive for the profitability of property and casualty reinsurance. That is what we saw happening in the marketplace.

To some extent, we can see the underlying logic of that kind of a reaction to an external development, but it takes us right back to our fundamental analysis of the reinsurance business. I served for some years as a director of a reinsurance company and, after maybe five years, I began to get some glimmers of how that strange and peculiar business functions. What it taught me was, from that experience, this was a real tough analytical problem to measure what the potential was in earning power of the reinsurance business, given the vagaries of that particular market.

But there are these kinds of events. We can all think of asbestos as a hugely negative impact on an array of companies with which we have never associated that hazard. Is it true that putting a communication receiver to your ear has an impact on the functioning of the brain? Was that write-down of market values that took place recently? Was that a scare? Was it valid? How do we know? Does anybody know? These kinds of questions are really hard to tell, whether developments in this category are really a trigger, a trigger that one really should respect and act upon.

One of the other kinds of developments that we have come to respect rationally, logically, and correctly is the takeover phenomenon. Much of the time, however, we focus on the target company, and we quite properly make our judgment on whether the intrinsic value of that company, plus a control premium, is adequately reflected in the anticipated takeover price and terms. But maybe we don't spend enough time on the impact of takeover developments on the prime mover, the organization that is engaging in the takeover.

We have some interesting studies on this subject generated in academia and elsewhere that raise lots of questions about how well designed and how well thought out [was the analysis of] the people engaging in the takeovers. Generally speaking, the conclusions of these not completely conclusive studies are: better to be the seller than the buyer in looking at those kinds of transactions.

This is to me a very explicit kind of an analytical problem. When you sit down carefully and think through the company before and after this acquisition, what has changed about its activities, about the characteristics of its earning power? What has happened in terms of the capital structure, which now allocates returns from the combined enterprise? These are all very good and demanding analytical studies. You cannot tell, in many instances, whether the acquiring company went through those kinds of analytical efforts or whether, in point of fact, we had simply an example of what we referred to as the agency problem,[5] where those in charge saw themselves as having a higher standing in their world by reason of leading a larger company than before, the wishful thinking that all managers have about their capacity to do more and to do it well, even though there may be a fundamental diversity in the characteristics of different lines of business.

Takeovers are a fascinating area of analysis. After the acquisition, you need to sit down all over again and think about what happened to the intrinsic value of this enterprise by reason of the acquisition, and you've got a big task. Those splendid financial statements that you will now see will have been doctored, and they will tell you a story that is contrary to fact. We combine all of the financial statements of the acquiring and the acquired companies, and we will take you back through past history, and it will tell you a story of a company that did not exist. And in the interest of comparability, they are saying to you, "Now, this is the way the company would have looked like had the merger and acquisition taken place five years ago." And you have to ask yourself, "What relevance does that information have?" The answer is probably very, very little.

There may be some ingredients of information about that line of business that you can go back and look through the acquired company and learn about. But the picture that ordinarily one looks at in those combined statements is, of course, a picture of nothing. It meets generally accepted accounting principles (GAAP) but probably has no analytical value of any kind. In fact, it may confuse you. It may, indeed, confuse you because it is like applying the history of one company and using it to anticipate the future of a different company.

We all know about takeovers and some of the postmortems that we all have in mind. Sometimes management's defense against a takeover was not a bad idea. In other cases, we wish their success had not been as effective.

As I finish up today, I would like to introduce you to a person that you might never have met before. Have you ever met a corporate director with twenty-three years of service who then proceeded in retirement to file shareholder resolutions?

The year in which these were filed, I was unable to find any instance but one. Think of a middle-sized company, market capitalization around $500 million. The directors have adopted a poison pill without, of course, consulting shareholders. Comes that retired director and introduces a resolution. What the board of directors should do is put the termination of the poison pill to a shareholder vote.[6] First year response, 40 percent in favor of that shareholder resolution, which you recognize immediately as a resounding outcome. Comes the second year, 47 and a fraction percent in favor of the resolution of submitting the poison pill to shareholders. Comes the next year, and we all know that you can win that kind of a resolution, and the board of directors can say, "Thank you very much. It was nice to hear from you, but they are not bound to take that action." But with 47 percent on your side, you've got a little something to negotiate with.

So you now address management and say, "Look, you stand a reasonable chance of losing that resolution. Would you rather do this a different way? A new procedure that will be tested this year after the annual meeting, distributed with the April dividend check, a shareholders survey?" We are going to take a survey of shareholders [to see] whether they are for or against the poison pill. You can vote for abolition of the poison pill, or its continuation, or undecided. You have the undecided provision in there so you can make sure you have a quorum, a third of the outstanding shares voted.

If the resolution to abolish the poison pill wins, the management is committed that they will, indeed, rescind it. You notice this is not in the proxy this time. It is in a shareholder survey with the understanding clear commitment that the outcome will be a directive which the board will follow. It means you don't have proxies. You don't write garbage in legalese to shareholders. The former director has his opportunity to write his piece, and it is not restricted to 500 words or some other gobbledygook like that.

Well, you have guessed by now that I am that former director. This may turn out to be a real nonevent. It may not carry the mail, but isn't it time that more than one former director filed a shareholder resolution? One year when I was still on the board, I had put in the proxy statement that I dissented for a particular provision in our executive incentive plan. Stock appreciation rights have always been to me one of the most inappropriate possible kinds of incentives for you to offer an executive who you want to be thoughtful about the role of the shareholder. You don't make him act like a shareholder as [would happen] with ordinary incentive stock options because you stop him out in the sense that he never has to put a dime at risk. He can just wait to enjoy the upside through his stock appreciation rights, when us poor shareholders have an opportunity to share fully in the bad news.

The point of mentioning this kind of strange and unusual behavior on the part of a long-term former director is to suggest that the agency problem, the lack of accountability of management and boards of directors to shareholders, is extremely widespread. Why have I been a missionary on this subject all these years? Simple reason. If the private sector, if investors and corporate managers, cannot deal with these kinds of decisions responsibly, you and I know that one day there will be some geniuses in our legislative processes who will be glad to take over that assignment and impose on our business system sets of requirements, regulations. And the one thing that we are fully aware of is that the burden of regulatory processes on so many activities of the private sector is a very significant burden on the competitiveness, effectiveness, and productivity of our private system on which we rely as the major contributor to a rising standard of living.

What does that have to do with these four lectures? Answer: the heart of the process and the attainments of our investment experience. Security analysts say, "Go away and leave me alone. I have enough problems doing my regular analytical work." My response is always coming back. What is your big stake? Your big stake is in the operation of the business system, the structure of private business decision making. Compared to that stake, much of what you are worrying about borders on the trivial. So one of the pieces of unfinished business, although I must say the signs of activity in this arena are very promising indeed, but one of the unfinished businesses is that ingredient of investment decision making which goes beyond short-term buy/sell kinds of decisions and valuations to the fundamental components of economic value, and there is where we are in need of a higher level of accountability for those making decisions in corporate enterprise.

Thank you for your attention and letting me make these closing remarks, which are right from the soapbox and not from the academic roster.

GABELLI: Roger, thank you. For those of you who want to know it, this is the cover of *Security Analysis*. It is the fifth edition, and Roger Murray is the author, and Roger, it is a little heavy, but as some of you don't know, Roger walks back from the Yale Club, and, even today, I told him, "Roger, I'm riding," and he made a major concession to his lifestyle and shared the cab with me. So, Roger, it is a little heavy, but on behalf of Gabelli Asset Management Company, thank you very much. On the back, we have the invitation that was sent to all of you in regard to this series of lectures, and I will just rest it here, Roger, but you can hold it for a moment if you would like.

MURRAY: Oh, it is heavy.

GABELLI: Now, within that context, in addition to understanding the dynamics of intrinsic value, price convergence, you also heard Roger start something that he didn't know he was going to start, and that is, the whole subject of accountability at the high level of management to look at the fundamental concepts of economic value. The agency problem, the poison pill, those things are interrelated.

Roger, I have a feeling that the Gabelli organization is going to sponsor a forum on the poison pill and maybe even allow you to use our organization to send a proposal to all companies to include on their proxy the elimination of the poison pill. We think that in a world in which the Berlin Wall was taken down, and where human values have been unleashed in terms of freedom, maybe there is a need for greater accountability than you see in the trend now in corporate America.

You touched on several of my key stocks here, Deere and American Express, and several of our companies that are present, about the whole concept of acquisitions, and what does it add to shareholder values. Maybe we can get you to take the PP test for corporate America, the Poison Pill test.

So, on behalf of all of us, security analysts today, the past, and the future, thanks very much, Roger, for sharing this with us.

Anyone that would like a tape, and we obviously have the Murray tapes, we will work with them and get them off to you.

PART THREE

INTERVIEW

14

FULL INTERVIEW WITH PETER J. TANOUS (1996)

In his book, *Investment Gurus*, published in 1997, Peter J. Tanous interviewed eighteen investment professionals, one of whom was Roger Murray. The following is an edited (for readability) reprint of the full interview, which took place in 1996. (Tanous published only a portion of the interview in his book.)

PETER TANOUS: Professor Murray, we always start off with one question, which is common to all the interviews, how did you first get interested in stocks?

ROGER MURRAY: As an undergraduate student at Yale, after taking my first economics course, I did a summer project for my instructor who then gave me some extra credit for Economics 101 by doing an analysis of several companies and their equity securities. This gave me a chance in the summer of 1930 to do my first analytical undertakings. Fortunately, no one was relying upon my conclusions. Although the Harvard Economic Society had informed us that the decline in economic activity had run its course by the middle of 1930, we found out later that it was only the beginning.

TANOUS: What year are we talking about?

MURRAY: I was doing this in the summer of 1930.

TANOUS: So, we're just talking months after the crash.

MURRAY: That's right.

TANOUS: At the start of the Great Depression, really.

MURRAY: That's right. But there was, in the spring of 1930, a widespread view that that market crash was behind us. And now that it was all over, we would resume long-term economic growth, and all was well. And the market rallied in the spring of 1930. What happened in 1931 was the British going off the gold standard and the collapse of the German banks, and all of those events were not at all visualized or foreseen. One of the securities I analyzed was Missouri Pacific Convertible Preferred Stock. I had a very good exercise in understanding and analyzing the conversion feature. The only trouble was the conversion feature was quite irrelevant when the stock was wiped out in the subsequent bankruptcy of the Missouri Pacific. That's how I got my first experience.

TANOUS: Even though you're very well known as an academic, professor, you didn't start out that way. In fact, you had an illustrious career in business before you became a full-time academic, didn't you?

MURRAY: Yes, I did. In the spring of 1932, if you had any hopes of getting married, you had to go to work if you could possibly find a job. I was happily able to do that. That enabled me to save enough money to get married in 1934.

TANOUS: So you were married in 1934, and where were you working?

MURRAY: I was working at the Bankers Trust Company. It was interesting in those days; you started for $25 a week and they assured you that you were being grossly overpaid because they really didn't need your services very badly. They were carrying old-time employees out of a sense of care and loyalty, but they did venture to take on three trainees in June 1932 instead of the usual thirty. And I was happily able to get one of those spots.

TANOUS: Now, at this point you had graduated from Yale, correct? And obviously with a great academic distinction because if you were one of three students picked out of thirty, just as the depression was about to start, I guess that's quite an achievement in itself, isn't it?

MURRAY: Well, I most certainly had great hesitation when I told the senior officer in the bank, would it be alright if I took two days off after graduation before I reported for work. I didn't want to appear to be casual about starting work. He assured me it was quite alright.

TANOUS: You got a whole two-day transition time to yourself before starting work.

MURRAY: That's right.

TANOUS: This is a little bit off the subject, but my father graduated from college in 1932, so I guess his experiences were similar. But a lot of your classmates just didn't find work, did they?

MURRAY: That's right. I had one of my very good friends and a very fine-looking colleague, who had been very active in drama and all kinds of things like that, and he was selling neckties at Macy's. And so I had to be careful to make sure that I didn't go through the necktie department and see him or have him see me coming by because he hardly needed recognition in that kind of a position.

TANOUS: What a story. Perhaps you can tell us about your transition from banking to academia.

MURRAY: I had earned my graduate degrees and worked my way up the ladder. I had a very happy experience at the bank. At the time when I was elected a vice president, I was the youngest vice president in the history of the bank. I had a very fine career there. Most enjoyable, most gratifying in all respects. I had known for many years Courtney Brown who had become the dean of Columbia Business School, after having been a colleague in my early days at Bankers Trust Company. He invited me to come as associate dean and kind of be the inside man when he was the outside dean responsible for fundraising and the like. Well, I hadn't had the experience of teaching a class for thirteen weeks and finding out two things. One, could I do it well? And, as we all know, you can't deceive yourself. If you don't do well in the classroom, you know it. There's no mistaking the fact that you've had a bad day or that you've had a good day in that classroom period. I went as associate dean, where I'd manage budgets and faculty recruiting and curriculum design and all those kinds of things, on condition that I could teach one course. I had already signed up to take the seminar which Benjamin Graham had taught for many years because he was retiring to California. I had already sat in on the seminar with him with great benefit and enjoyment. But that wasn't the same as teaching a class. That was just a fun experience, watching and listening to one of the masters of the field. My understanding with Dean Brown was that I would continue [teaching] that one class each semester while doing my administrative tasks as associate dean. He agreed cheerfully and I had two and a half years in which I could find out the answer to those questions. Could I teach? Did I really like it and find it rewarding? And when the answers turned out to be affirmative, I stood for tenure. I had a wonderful team of professors examining me. I had done a lot of writing in my work as chief economist at Bankers Trust Company and related lines, so I could meet the publication standard and the recognition of colleagues in the field.

TANOUS: Indeed. It's staggering to think that you're talking about taking classes with Benjamin Graham. What was [David] Dodd's role at the time?

MURRAY: He [Dodd] taught the security analysis course. He had done that for a couple of decades, right from the text [*Security Analysis*]. The text was an interesting joint product. Ben Graham was not addicted to writing a serious text. He loved ideas, loved to chat, loved to think out loud. Dave Dodd sat in Ben's classes and took copious notes. Then Dodd would go and dig out and verify the background from the examples that Ben had used, and that's how the first edition in 1934 got put together. In 1934, the conventional wisdom was that bonds were the only investment outlet.

TANOUS: Is that right?

MURRAY: Stocks were nothing but speculation. Pure and simple. The mission that Ben and Dave had in doing the first edition [of *Security Analysis*] was to say, "Now really? There is such a thing as investing in common stocks," contrary to the standard textbook on investments, which in those days was by Chamberlain.[1] They made it absolutely clear that the stocks were speculation; bond investing was the only avenue that could be called investing. After the devastating carnage of the securities markets, nobody was prepared, except Graham and Dodd, to stand up and say, "Now just a darn minute. When those prices get low enough, even what you might think of sheer speculative kinds of securities do have investment quality" because you are paying a price that provides you with, to use their term, a big margin of safety.

TANOUS: And that presumably is the value stock thesis, is it?

MURRAY: Value stock thesis, that's right.

TANOUS: As I understand it actually you taught after Graham.

MURRAY: When Dave Dodd retired in 1961, I had been at Columbia for half a dozen years, I took his class and, from then on, I taught the security analysis course.

TANOUS: And, of course, you're the coauthor of the most recent edition of the book [fifth edition], or are you not?

MURRAY: That's right. When I had started teaching, [I taught] from the edition of the 1950s. For the 1962 edition, I was the publisher's adviser. So when Ben Graham and Sydney Cottle were doing that edition, I had the fun of being a kind of arbiter or settler of the debates between them.

TANOUS: You were the kibitzer.

MURRAY: Yeah, I was the kibitzer. I had stored up from that experience and, of course, from teaching lots of ideas that I had an opportunity to develop more in the 1988 fifth edition.

TANOUS: I can't resist asking you, what Graham and Dodd were like as people.

MURRAY: Ben was just exactly the way I think he is, generally, pictured. A man of great breadth of background, fine classic scholar. A man with an idea a minute. If you hadn't visited with him for a while, first thing you know you were exploring all kinds of avenues either directly or not at all directly related to security selection. Just a wonderfully agile mind. Dave Dodd, wonderful gentleman. Just one of the finest people I ever met anywhere. He could listen to Ben all day long, but he retained a healthy skepticism and when Ben would launch on one of his ideas that came along about every thirty seconds, Dave would just quietly sit down and say, "That's an interesting idea, Ben; however, I don't believe that the facts really support that strong a conclusion." And then he would get to work on the serious analysis.

TANOUS: But these guys would sit around and come up with investment ideas?

MURRAY: They just loved to talk about their experiences. They were the early investors in Geico. They were always kind of interested in insurance companies because insurance companies had portfolios of assets. And, as you know, Warren Buffett—

TANOUS: No, I was going to ask you—

MURRAY: "Where does he get all his assets?" He generated them in the insurance business. Of course, we think it's Berkshire Hathaway, but most of the time it's one of their insurance companies that owns large parts of that portfolio. That business lends itself to financial analysis. Obviously on the underwriting side. But you become the manager of large amounts of capital, which, if you stay in property and casualty insurance, is going to be predominantly equity money. And so it was natural for these kinds of people who demonstrate that fundamental financial analysis, by which they mean, of course, where you take financial statements that people prepare to give the best possible picture of their enterprise. You take them apart and you find out what the enterprise is really like.

TANOUS: Right, as long as you're talking insurance, I'm curious about how, from a value-investing point of view, you deal with the underwriting risk such as three hurricanes.

MURRAY: As you know, Buffett deals with it in its most extreme form in the insurance.

TANOUS: So you lay off the risk basically.

MURRAY: One can systematically analyze levels of experience and exposure, now it doesn't mean you end up with certainty, but if you do your homework, you will end up in that kind of a business, just like managing a portfolio with a margin of safety. That term shows up so frequently in Graham and Dodd.

TANOUS: The reinsurance really answers my question about the insurance. You just lay off the risk to somebody else, right?

MURRAY: That's right. Make sure that you keep control of your exposure.

TANOUS: I have got to ask you: at Columbia, you did run across this bright young kid called Warren Buffett?

MURRAY: He had come and gone before I got there. I didn't meet him until later. A good session I had with him was when we were both on the SEC [(U.S.) Securities and Exchange Commission] Advisory Committee on corporate disclosure, which was a great fun enterprise to get on. An absolutely top-flight group of lawyers, accountants, security analysts, and investors. Start from ground zero and say, "What are the objectives and what have we achieved in the area of disclosure of financial information?"

TANOUS: That's when you and he got together?

MURRAY: That's when we had gotten together because I'd been introduced by Dave Dodd. This is one of the times where we could sit around the table and really discuss these things at length.

TANOUS: Have you had any other relationship with him?

MURRAY: He's come back to Columbia. When I taught the class in value analysis, the year before last, he was one of our guest speakers. You heard about that class, have you?

TANOUS: Could you remind me?

MURRAY: We did it right out of the blue. We undertook to teach a seminar limited to seventy-five kids, but we had applications of upwards of 200, in value investing. Because you discover in our wonderful world of quantitative methods and financial economics, the students don't have much opportunity to explore areas like this.

TANOUS: Why not?

MURRAY: Well, it's interesting. I'm currently serving on a group for the CFA Institute. We're looking for the kind of training that a specialist in equity investing should have. They finished the CFA; they are still actively engaged in equity security selection and portfolio management. What should we offer them beyond what's covered in the CFA program? And it's fascinating. It's about a dozen of us working on this, and there are two of us who are paying some attention to accounting and corporate finance. And what are the rest of them focusing on? Valuation. I always come back to something that Ben Graham said to me when we were visiting after the seminar was over. He said, "If you give me a reliable estimate of the earnings power of a company, I'll value it on the back of an envelope."

TANOUS: I think even growth managers would agree with that.

MURRAY: You can see the difference in emphasis. The emphasis today is on which valuation model you prefer, or you think is more effective, or you think is more effective for growth versus value, versus the stress test, versus private companies, versus whatever particular investment question you're asking. And that's the focus. And what the modern technology enables us to do is take those provided streams of data and test them, use them to test alternative models or variations in models. This is the old formula: garbage in, garbage out. Use inaccurate, misleading, inconsistent kinds of financial information, and reframe it, process it extensively through your best advanced quantitative methods and you will end up with, in my humble opinion, an unreliable, potentially seriously inaccurate conclusion.

TANOUS: What's an example of that?

MURRAY: I would say that when I sit down and look at a company that has had an active process of acquisitions, and I press the button and I get the data for the last five years, or ten years, which has been processed to give me a pro forma set of financial statements for a company that never existed. And now I am supposed to use that as a guide to what I should be expecting of this company that now does exist or is in the process of going through a transition into a new company. And I believe that to the extent that I rely on that historical information, I'm going to come up with a bum answer.

TANOUS: Why?

MURRAY: Because it's telling me the history that relates to a company that never existed and certainly will not exist in the future.

TANOUS: Why did we do this in the first place?

MURRAY: We do this presumably because we are saying it's hard to make reliable forecasts. There's a lot of evidence that, or most of us in this vale of tears, the pattern that has been established in the present and in the recent past is a better predictor of future outcomes than you, Murray, will be able to come up with.

TANOUS: True or false?

MURRAY: Well, that's what people are concluding.

TANOUS: Yeah, but you don't believe that do you?

MURRAY: Of course, I don't. But I say, "Of course, that's true if you're not willing to do your homework." Because what we're interested in is change. What changes will take place, we think, over the next three to five years or longer that are not anticipated by the present market price?

TANOUS: Now we're getting to the heart of this thing. I need to focus our discussion a little bit, if you don't mind, on one of the principal features of this book [*Securities Analysis*]. It's time to put the boxing gloves on. What we're doing is talking to a lot of active managers and, as you know, some academics. And I should add parenthetically that I am extremely grateful to Mario Gabelli for suggesting, in his shy and inimitable style that "you're talking to the wrong academics."

MURRAY: [laughs]

TANOUS: He said, "You haven't talked to Roger Murray." And I said, "Give me his number, I'm dying to talk to Roger Murray. I'd love to talk to Roger Murray." So I am grateful to the shy, retiring Mario for this because here's our conundrum. I have got a bunch of academics who are all efficient market theorists, who go on and on, two of them, as you know, won the Nobel Prize, and for all I know, Eugene Fama is on the list. Plus, Rex Sinquefield, who is not an academic, but he sure sounds like one. He's chairman of Dimensional Fund Advisors. And these guys, sort of, snicker when you talk about, you know, we're going to go out and analyze companies and we're going to figure out which ones have hidden values because, of course, there are no hidden values. Everything about that company is reflected in the market price. So please help me out.

MURRAY: To use the Graham and Dodd terminology, we're talking about the difference between intrinsic value and market value. Now market efficiency purists will tell you fundamentally the only real expression of value that exists is what you read in the market price. And it is the best expression, absent inside information, of the significant events that are occurring and are about to occur. That's saying the market price is the best estimate of economic value. Now, let's turn to the concept of intrinsic value, in a Graham and Dodd sense. This is the value of an enterprise. It's not a value of stock certificates; it's the value of a company, the value of a company based on its earnings power. What do we mean by earnings power? It's what we have a valid reason to expect, to anticipate in terms of the volume and profitability of the business and the characteristics of its lines of business. If we can identify those underlying characteristics, we can then reach some reliability conclusions about what may lie ahead in all of those terms, both consistency and levels of profitability.

TANOUS: Okay.

MURRAY: If we can do that, we don't have any problem on valuation. We don't need a choice of any one of six models, and we don't need to refine that estimate of value to three decimal places. What we're looking for is under- and overvaluation, recognizing what we've got inevitably is a margin of error in framing our expectations because we're talking about a future about which we only have vague knowledge and guidelines.

TANOUS: Okay, but absent the ability to predict the future, all of the information that leads to a valuation, say the efficient market theorists, is all out there, and it all comes to rest at one spot, which is the price at which the security trades. To them, there's no such thing as overvalued and undervalued because there's no such thing as missed priced securities.

MURRAY: Which, of course, is perfectly obviously a silly statement. How can you say there is no evidence of security being missed priced? Let's go back and look at our most recent history of the most efficient market. Let's start on January 1, 1995. I'll say all those securities are efficiently priced. And at the end of 1995, they trade at prices 35 percent higher.

TANOUS: Right, that's new information coming into the market.

MURRAY: New information? Was it really? Look at the underlying information: we had a very good year. Was it 17 percent? I don't know which measure you use. If you want to talk about new information, you could say, "Well, on average, we get only a 7 percent per annum increase in earnings, and this year it was 17 percent. The new information was the differential of 10 percent, right? Okay. How do you relate that to a 35 percent rise in price?

TANOUS: I don't know. How do you?

MURRAY: Well, you got to say that is not my idea of efficiency, and it isn't yours either when you sold out on the first of January. The other thing that happened, to your amazement, it made a difference what securities you had in your portfolio. If the market is efficient, it doesn't matter. You don't really need to diversify.

TANOUS: That's right. Well, you buy the market.

MURRAY: We know you want to avoid extreme economic, political, and other factors, but generally speaking, if General Motors is priced efficiently, it doesn't matter whether you buy General Motors or you buy Ford.

TANOUS: But then you don't have the benefit of diversification.

MURRAY: Well, I don't want to stake my whole future on the automobile business, so I will own General Motors or Ford, or both for heaven sakes. And then I will not have more than a 5 or 6 percent of my portfolio in the automobile business. But we're now talking about diversifying economic effects, industrial characteristics of global competition, and the like, of those factors. But these are all elements subject to the analytical process. Pursuing the case, why can market prices be so efficiently determined in such a highly developed market system?

TANOUS: Okay, that's a good question. What's the answer?

MURRAY: The answer is, they aren't because, really, wouldn't you rather make your decisions the easy way rather than the hard way?

TANOUS: Define please.

MURRAY: The easy way is saying, "I will just look around at reported earnings. I'm with the SEC: I think they ought to discontinue publishing footnotes in their financial statements. They just clutter up the thing with too much information. There's only one thing I need to know, and that's earnings per share."

TANOUS: Right, that's the easy way.

MURRAY: Tell me about momentum, won't you please? Anyway, it makes sense. The securities that show the best momentum will have the most promising future. But, you know, just ask yourself, what kind of reasoning is that? Momentum analysis means that you will miss every turning point in the course of a company's history.

TANOUS: You just hop on the train while it's roaring.

MURRAY: That's exactly right. You're late getting in and you're late getting out, so you tend to be buying at a premium and selling at a discount. You know, it's like the guys who use relative strength.

TANOUS: Yeah, exactly.

MURRAY: Exactly the same kind of a process. What do you really want to do? You really want to have the capacity to identify change, departures from the past pattern. And one thing you know about the past pattern of published financial statements is that there is a chief financial officer whose job is to smooth out as many of the bumps and provide as much continuity in a pattern of growth as you can. Now, we're talking about people who obey the law. We're not talking about fraud.

TANOUS: Yes, of course.

MURRAY: We're talking about the techniques within the range of generally accepted accounting principles that permit you to change the timing of the recognition of gains and losses. You can futz around with this stuff, but eventually the whole story will show up in those financial statements. But in the meantime, it's quite possible to change the pattern and what is the direction of that change in the published statements.

TANOUS: This presumably is the hard way, where you have to do the work to find out the data that's going to help you make an investment decision, right?

MURRAY: Exactly. Think of that financial statement as a published photographic portrait, where the guy has touched it up. He's taken out the blemishes. He's taken out the worry lines and a few things like that, and he gives you that lovely smooth picture. That's what the chief financial officer's assignment is.

TANOUS: That's what he wants you to see.

MURRAY: That's what he wants you to see. What I have said for years and years until I'm tired of hearing myself say it: every large corporation should have on the payroll a most highly skilled security analyst. Put him to work. Give him full access to all of the financial information being generated. Have him do a very down-to-earth, careful analysis where you don't have any of the sugarcoating or the fading out of blemishes. And have him work in secret.

TANOUS: Okay.

MURRAY: And you as the chief executive of this company, in your locked bottom desk drawer, have his analytical results. Look at them instead of what those wonderful financial people are saying or what the investor relations people are saying and what your PR people are saying. You would make much better decisions for your company if you saw it as it really is instead of as it has been touched up.

TANOUS: Well, what's the role of the auditor in all this?

MURRAY: The auditor has no basis for a complaint. You are still within the range of generally accepted accounting principles. Just think of the financial statements we have been reading in the last five years [interview took place in 1996]. This is after one of the great inflationary periods in American economic history. This is after a major change in the price level has had its opportunity to work its way through the system. Under these circumstances, we will be looking at huge amounts of realized capital gains on capital assets. Pick an industry. Of course, they will come to fruition. And what do we read instead? You don't find any unusual gains realized. All you're reading about is unusual capital losses.

TANOUS: That's right. The assets are valued at cost, right? And, of course, if they don't sell them, they are just there, right?

MURRAY: And they're just there, and if you do sell them, they will show a big profit. And yet you and I look at those restructuring write-offs and now we have this new one about how you write down long-lived assets that seem to have lost value, and they're these huge write-offs. Now what does that tell you? It tells you that we have had a huge overstatement of corporate earnings power.

TANOUS: I'm sorry, I didn't follow that.

MURRAY: There has been a totally inadequate level of appreciation for the expiration of economic value, and what we have failed to do is to recognize the reality that we don't use up capital assets. They simply lose value because of obsolescence from various sources. Now, in determining the intrinsic value of an enterprise is to try and get at the real earnings power, not reported earnings power, but the actual economic value of that company.

TANOUS: Got it. Which the market may or may not perceive correctly?

MURRAY: Exactly. We can say, with a high degree of certainty, the market is going to be right in lots of valuations of lots of companies. It may be by chance. It may be a random event. But one of the things that the trained security analyst has to do is develop a willingness to throw away his work. You go to work and you think you have a scent of undervaluation. You do all your work and your best conclusion is, "No, it's not undervalued. It's fairly valued in the marketplace."

TANOUS: Throw it out.

MURRAY: And now you say, "Well, I learned something, but isn't this terrible?" You and I know many analysts will say if they come up with that answer, "I must have missed something."

TANOUS: Yeah. I'll find a reason to buy it anyway.

MURRAY: Absolutely. Absolutely. With all this effort—

TANOUS: I can't waste all this time.

MURRAY: Exactly.

TANOUS: I want to ask you, from an individual investor point of view. He'll be bombarded, particularly after a year like 1995, where the vast majority of mutual funds and investors did not do as well as the market. He might just throw in the towel and say, you know, "What the hell? Why don't I buy an index fund or a combination of index funds rather than try to do all this myself?" What advice would you have for that investor?

MURRAY: I would say go ahead and buy that diversified portfolio. Make your choices about the type of asset allocation that you're making. Focus on asset allocation.

TANOUS: That's, of course, the Brinson[, Hood,] Beebower study,[2] which everybody's looking at now.

MURRAY: Yeah, because the big difference in your returns will come on your asset allocation decision.

TANOUS: Right.

MURRAY: Most of us, unless, you have some real skill and you're really ready to work.

TANOUS: Well, you think it might be okay for an individual investor to buy markets as opposed to stocks or managers?

MURRAY: Yes, I do. Because . . . on a part-time basis . . . most people don't have the time or the expertise to make informed choices.

TANOUS: Yeah, good point. I interviewed Peter Lynch and of course I read all his books. Peter Lynch basically says, you know, go hang at the mall, see where the lines are longest, just do a little research and you might find a great company.

MURRAY: What Peter says about that is perfectly good sense. This is one of the oldest dimensions of security analysis. Where do you begin your security analysis? By looking at the company. What's its trade position? What's its competitive environment? What are the costs of entry? All of those factors that investors are beginning to discover, which I thought I learned as a graduate student. But that doesn't take you the last mile. If you go through that kind of process, you do that kind of sorting, and you say to yourself, "I've studied retailing intensively, and I believe that the discount store is here to stay. So I'm going to make my long-term investment in Kmart."

TANOUS: Yeah, bad choice.

MURRAY: Now, I did everything right, up to the point of analyzing Kmart versus Walmart.

TANOUS: Well, all right. Let me ask you this. Let's say I'm the investor and I say, "Professor, I really appreciate your advice and you're right. What the heck. My odds aren't too good since I'm not a professional investor. Maybe I should just buy these index funds. But I want to tell you something. I want to confide in you. I really am prepared to do the work. I mean, I'm really into this thing. Give me some advice on beating the market and selecting some of these great undervalued securities."

MURRAY: I say, you sit down and think your way all through where you are going to identify your universe. You've heard Warren Buffett say many times, "I don't make my choices in fields that I don't understand." That's a very good line of advice, to stay away from not only activities that are unfamiliar to you but will continue to be unfamiliar to you. That's the first level of advice. The second level of advice is, by the time a company has its highest level of recognition and popularity, you can be pretty darn sure that the market valuation has run well in excess of the intrinsic value of the company when it's that well known and that well liked.

TANOUS: So you got to find the undiscovered ones. Is that what you're saying?

MURRAY: Find the undiscovered one. Look at a field that makes good sense on business and economic grounds. Then bore your way through the whole battery of information on companies that are in that field and who have got themselves established to some extent. Now sit down and do an old-fashioned spreadsheet comparative analysis. What's happening? Look at all the companies in this field, and you've narrowed it down to six established companies. Now sit down and put them through your ratio analysis. It gives you some insights from that, assuming now you're satisfied that the data you're using are not misleading and are consistently comparable enough so that your comparisons have a chance of being meaningful. See rates of change and the level of stability in the underlying earnings power of that array of companies and narrow yourself down from six to two.

TANOUS: Got it. And how about buying them both?

MURRAY: You may even buy them both. You may have narrowed them down to two. Having now investigated them further, having tried to learn more about them, you may decide that this looks like too close to call, so I'll put half my money in each.

TANOUS: That sounds terrific. I want to ask you about your role with the individual retirement account [IRA]. Could you tell me about that?

MURRAY: I had been Gene Keogh's[3] expert for—

TANOUS: Who is Gene Keogh? I know the Keogh Plan, but who is Gene Keogh?

MURRAY: He was the member of the House Ways and Means Committee from Brooklyn. Because he was from Brooklyn and he was a fairly senior guy on the Ways and Means Committee, when he called the chairman of the Bankers Trust Company and said, "I need an expert to support me against the Treasury's contention that the Keogh Act will be too expensive, too great a revenue loss." And the chairman said, "I know just the guy you want to talk to. His name is Roger Murray." And for ten years, each year, when the bill would come up, one year in the House Ways and Means, next year in the Senate Finance Committee, I would go [to Washington] and give my testimony that the Treasury's estimates of revenue loss were absolutely unreal and outrageous. So anyway, we finally got it passed. I worked for ten years. I was at CREF [College Retirement Equities Fund] with a high level of exposure to pension benefits that were completely portable. One of the great assets of academia is that you can move and your retirement benefits will move right with you as long as you're in TIAA-CREF because you're holding the policy. It's always yours from day one.

TANOUS: Interesting.

MURRAY: I looked around the landscape and I said, We've got a fine organization here that covers academia. We have plans wherever there is
an organized company plan or an organized group from a labor union
or somebody else. But the one people in the world who don't have any
comparable opportunity are people who have a lifetime of work where
their economic asset is their skill and their professional ability and the
like, but they do not have a continuity of specific employment. What we
ought to do is to fill that gap by having an individual retirement account
[IRA] where the guy could sign up a financial institution and have a part
of his pay go, either by his employer's action or by his own action, into
that lifetime savings account. It would then be possible to do that and
have it tax deductible, just as it is for everybody else in public or private
pension arrangements. The beauty of this is that it becomes a wonderful asset for financial institutions, and they will promote it because they
will have a long-earned depositor that doesn't withdraw.

TANOUS: Exactly.

MURRAY: And furthermore, here is the ideal place for people to buy stocks
and make long-term equity investing because they will have locked
themselves in through this program. The one thing we know about
stocks is that they're illiquid. They're a lousy short-term investment.
But if you give me fifteen or twenty years, I'll give you a superior rate of
total return, which is what you need for your retirement savings.

TANOUS: The idea sounds great, is great. How did we get from your cogi-
tating about this idea to the IRA as we know it today?

MURRAY: There was a hearing in Washington and they were kind enough
to invite me to come to talk about retirement income and gaps in it, and
I gave what I thought was excellent testimony.

TANOUS: I am sure it was.

MURRAY: Nobody gave me the time of day.

TANOUS: What?

MURRAY: Got nowhere.

TANOUS: Really?

MURRAY: However, the Hunt Commission was appointed to study our
financial institutions, and the Hunt Commission invited me because of
what I'd written and done in the field of pensions, to write them a paper.
What they asked for is . . . we don't want a research paper. We've got
all the research papers in the world. What we want is a position paper,
and in the position that you are expected to address, how do we cure
the maintenance of fiduciary standards for the protection of pension

promises? And I said, "I'm delighted. I'm just the right guy to do that." So here comes the paper on protecting fiduciary standards in the administration of pension plans. But curiously enough, as you get about two-thirds of the way through the paper, we have a slight departure. We talk about the gap and the availability of pension plans of the individual not part of a significant group. And the potential remedy for this is a thing called an individual retirement account. Well, they had a crackerjack group of research people for the Hunt Commission. They had me in for a discussion, and I met with them. We talked a little bit about protection, and then we shifted to the individual retirement account. And they said, "Hey, you've really got something. You're absolutely right." We talked some more about it and they developed it. They submitted it to the Hunt Commission and the Hunt Commission says, "Great. You're quite right. Your argument is well made. And this is what we ought to recommend." So out of the Hunt Commission report comes ERISA, the Employee Retirement Income Security Act.

TANOUS: Oh, the ERISA.

MURRAY: Where do you find a tax benefit for the self-employed or for the individual employee? Answer: an ERISA. It's ERISA that provides you with the deductibility of your contribution to an IRA. Never happened in the history of mankind. This is a tax bill. It's a revenue bill. And [ERISA] gets put into a bill for the careful inspection and auditing of fiduciary standards of pension plans.

TANOUS: That's very interesting. And so, of course, it was the ERISA bill then, right?[4]

MURRAY: It got in the ERISA bill, got in the act. I don't know of any other case where a tax benefit is included in revenue legislation. But the magic here was that this could happen, not in ten or twelve years, like the Keogh Act, but like in three or four [years]. Because it got into ERISA and that had enough priority to get signed on Labor Day in 1974 and, lo and behold, this retirement tax feature got included.

TANOUS: And we have you to thank for it.

MURRAY: We got in the side door.

TANOUS: You got in the side door, that's okay.

MURRAY: Yeah.

TANOUS: Professor, I guess I'm getting down to the last question, but one thing that occurs to me is that the coincidence of your signing this bill just as we came to the end of the '73 to '74 bear market is a little striking, don't you think?

MURRAY: Yeah, that's right. It was by sheer accident, sheer coincidence. Because I had done work on pension reform and stuff like that way back in the sixties. First appointment I had was from when Kennedy was in office. And I worked on one of the task forces that addressed pension reform. But it took a long time and a long series of hearings and discussions and everything else to finally get to the question.

TANOUS: Yeah.

MURRAY: By happenstance, the best piece I ever wrote and the one that got perhaps one of the widest circulations was a September 1974 report for the annual report of the Common Fund. That's a fun story that you might enjoy. What was happening in the Common Fund was that colleges and universities were withdrawing their participation in the equity fund, and we knew where it was going. It was going to those high-yield returns in the bond market. And so we said, "We've got to do something." And so, "Let's get together and write a statement. Roger, you write the first draft." Oh, I wrote the first draft and we had a meeting of the investment committee. We went all over it, and they said, "Gee, well, we like this, we kind of agree with it, but we think you're taking too strong a position" because my position was that this is the opportunity of a lifetime, to buy equities.

TANOUS: This is in 1974 we're talking?

MURRAY: This is September 1974. The timing was so good because we had a June 30 fiscal year and a late September annual meeting. But anyway, we got together, and they all wanted to tone it down. I listened patiently. I said, "Tell you what? I've got a deal you can't refuse. I'll write a disclaimer. I'll say this is not really an expression of the Common Fund. We observe the freedom of thinking and speech common to academia. So this is one man's opinion, not necessarily endorsed by the trustees." My offer was, I said, "Look, if this is right, this'll be the Common Fund's statement." If it turns out to be wrong, say, "That's what Murray said. You remember our disclaimer there."

TANOUS: It's great. Did it work?

MURRAY: It worked. I went back to my original draft and didn't have to modify the conclusions. It was illustrative of the conventional wisdom. I never had more invitations to go speak than I had in the fall of 1974. They couldn't get anybody else. They didn't think I was so great, but they couldn't get anybody else.

TANOUS: To talk about investing in the market?

MURRAY: To talk constructively about buying equities.

TANOUS: That's amazing.

MURRAY: It was a kind of one-man survey I did. And I'll never forget: I had never spoken at the Chicago Analysts Society, and here comes an invitation from one of my old friends who knew where I stood. "Won't you come out and talk to us?" And I said, "Well, I'd be delighted." And that was the only time I ever used the word *never*. You know the old saying, never use the word *never* in relation to equities? And I used the word, "You'll never have an opportunity to buy stocks as cheap as they are now."

TANOUS: Wow.

MURRAY: One of my old friends said, "Say, I've heard you say lots of times never say never, but you said it." And I said, "Yes, I said it and I meant it." Because on an analytical basis, there's no question. It didn't tell you that the market couldn't go down another 5 percent or 10 percent or 20 percent or whatever. But this was an absolute steal.

TANOUS: Well, you know, you're inviting me to ask you, you're making it impossible for me not to ask you, What do you think about buying equities in mid-1996 [the time of the interview]?

MURRAY: In mid-1996 they are overvalued. The case is not as extreme as in 1987, but it's only not as extreme because we do not have the interest rate factor as strongly positioned as it was in 1987. And in 1987, I got every one of my pension asset management clients to cut the equity exposure by 20 percentage or 25 percentage points.

TANOUS: What would you do today [in 1996]?

MURRAY: Today, I would get back to the minimum part of your range. My typical pension fund range is 50 percent to 75 percent. Don't worry if you run over, don't rebalance unless you cross 80 percent. But if that's really your range, and none of them really have a 50 percent bottom, it's much closer to 60 percent, you ought to be down close to your minimum. But my minimum is higher than lots of people's.

TANOUS: Well, of course, because you know market timing doesn't really pay. I want to ask you one last question, Professor. First of all, do you mind if I mention your age in the interview?

MURRAY: I'm not sensitive to it. Obviously, if you think about my experience, I graduated from college in 1932 even though I was not quite twenty-one, it's not hard to figure.

TANOUS: No, you're right. I'm glad you're not sensitive about it because I think it adds greatly to this wisdom. And, in fact, this is probably going to be the longest interview in the book but deservedly so.

MURRAY: One of the interesting things that I have reflected on, I don't know whether this is of interest to you, but how have I been such a chronic buyer of equities. As soon as I got out of the bank and could borrow money, particularly in times like 1974, I would always buy stocks. How come somebody who had full exposure to the Great Depression could turn out to be—

TANOUS: Such a bull?

MURRAY: Always a bull.

TANOUS: I'm going to ask that question and make myself smart.

MURRAY: Well, the answer is, if you went through that period and you were, as I was, an MBA or a PhD candidate, and I was immersed in those financial markets and in the economic environment, after you had been through that [the Great Depression], the kinds of worries and concerns that have baffled investors and market makers in the fifties, sixties, seventies, eighties, and nineties are trivia.

TANOUS: Well said. Professor, thank you very much. I think we'll end it there. I'm so grateful to you. This is so rich in everything I want it to be. And I'm grateful to Mario [Gabelli] as well.

MURRAY: Oh, it's fun to talk about these things.

TANOUS: It really is, and I'm so glad I got a prominent academic who was not an efficient market theorist because it's very important to—

MURRAY: One of the nice things that happened to me, I don't know whether you're familiar, is the Nicholas Molodovsky Award.

TANOUS: No. I didn't.

MURRAY: It's the highest award given. It's been given ten times since 1968. Bill Sharpe had it.

TANOUS: What's it called?

MURRAY: The Nicholas Molodovsky Award. And that was the nicest thing. The first recipient, of course, was, Molodovsky. The third [recipient] was Benjamin Graham.

TANOUS: That's good company.

MURRAY: And the most recent is Marty Lebowitz, one of the greats. Anyway, honorary degrees are nice, and they say nice things about you, but this, in many ways, was my highlight. This award is presented periodically only to those individuals who have made outstanding contributions of such significance as to change the direction of the profession.

TANOUS: Now I notice it on your bio. It has AIMR on there. What's the connection?

MURRAY: They make the award, one of their committees.

TANOUS: Oh, I see. It's the New York Society of Security Analysts.

MURRAY: This is the national organization. The Association for Investment Management and Research [AIMR].

TANOUS: Whose standards, obviously, we want everybody to follow in performance measurement.

MURRAY: Yeah, that's right. That's the nicest that happened. It was nice to join that long list.

TANOUS: And, well, indeed and I'll not fail to mention it. Professor, thank you so much for this interview.

BIBLIOGRAPHY OF ROGER MURRAY'S PUBLICATIONS

Roger F. Murray, "A Program of Financial Research," Nation Bureau of Economic Research, Bulletin 64 (May 1937): 2–22.

Roger F. Murray, "Regulation of Airline Securities," *Harvard Business Review* (1949): 71–76.

Roger F. Murray, "The Impact of Federal Taxes and Controls on Corporate Profit Margins," *The Analysts Journal* 7, no. 1 (First Quarter 1951): 49–50.

Roger F. Murray, "Investment Aspects of the Accumulation of Pension Funds," *The Journal of Finance* 7, no. 2 (May 1952): 252–59.

Roger F. Murray, "Federal Debt Management and the Institutional Investor," *Law and Contemporary Problems* 17, no. 1 (Winter 1952): 198–218.

Roger F. Murray, "Trusts and Mutual Savings Banks," *The Analysts Journal* 9, no. 3 (June 1953): 72–74.

Roger F. Murray, "New Life in the Corporate Bond Market," *The Analysts Journal* 9, no. 5 (November 1953): 13–15.

Roger F. Murray, "What Yield Do You Use?," *The Analysts Journal* 11, no. 4 (August 1955): 15–16.

Roger F. Murray, "Interest Rates and Their Influence of Equity Prices," *The Analysts Journal* 12, no. 3 (June 1956): 15–17.

Roger F. Murray, "Institutional Influences on the Stock Market," *The Analysts Journal* 14, no. 2 (May 1958): 15–16.

Roger F. Murray, "The Outlook for the Stock Market," *The Journal of Finance* 18, no. 2 (May 1963): 410–12.

Roger F. Murray, "The Market for Equities," *The Journal of Finance* 19, no. 2 (May 1964): 417–19.

Roger F. Murray, "Quality and Liquidity at a Discount," *Financial Analysts Journal* 20, no. 4 (July–August 1964): 114–15.

Roger F. Murray, "Urgent Questions About the Stock Market," *Harvard Business Review* (September–October 1964): 53–59.

Roger F. Murray, "A Yardstick to Measure Pension Fund Performance," Bank Administration Institute (1968): 50, 92.

Roger F. Murray, "Economic Aspects of Pensions: A Summary Report," National Bureau of Economic Research (NBER), 1968.

Roger F. Murray, "Pension Funds in the American Economy," *The Journal of Finance* 23, no. 2 (May 1968): 331–36.

Roger F. Murray, "The Future of Private Pensions: Some Economic Aspects," *The Journal of Risk and Insurance* 34, no. 1 (March 1969): 27–32.

Roger F. Murray, "An Overview of the Life Insurance–Mutual Fund Combination," *The Journal of Risk and Insurance* 36, no. 4 (September 1969): 419–24.

Roger F. Murray, "The Penn Central Debacle: Lessons for Financial Analysis," *The Journal of Finance* 26, no. 2 (May 1971): 327–32.

Roger F. Murray, "Institutionalization of the Stock Market: To Be Feared or Favored?," *Financial Analysts Journal* 30, no. 2 (March–April 1974): 18–20, 22.

Roger F. Murray, "A New Role for Options," *The Journal of Financial and Quantitative Analysis* 14, no. 4 (November 1979): 895–99.

Roger F. Murray, "Graham and Dodd: A Durable Discipline," *Financial Analysts Journal* 40, no. 5 (September–October 1984): 18–19, 22–23.

NOTES

A PERSONAL TRIBUTE TO PROFESSOR ROGER MURRAY

1. Elizabeth Humphrey, "Exploring the Underground with Mark Rudd '69," *Columbia College Today*.

2. "The Whiz Kids," *Forbes*, October 15, 2001.

3. James Russell Kelly, "Roger F. Murray: The Bridge between Benjamin Graham and Modern Value Investing," *Financial History* 133 (Spring 2020): 25–27, 39.

PREFACE

1. Special thanks to James Kelly for providing the metaphor.

INTRODUCTION

1. The first lecture, along with the three other lectures, are printed in their entirety in part 2 of this text.

2. Roger F. Murray, *Lectures Held at the Museum of Television and Radio in New York* (Rye, NY: Gabelli Asset Management Co., 1993), lecture 1.

3. Murray, *Lectures*, lecture 1.

4. Murray, *Lectures*, lecture 1.

5. Kathleen Broome Williams, *Grace Hopper: Admiral of the Cyber Sea* (Annapolis, MD: Naval Institute Press, 2013), 2.

6. Williams, *Grace Hopper*, 2–6.

7. Williams, *Grace Hopper*, 7.

8. Williams, *Grace Hopper*, 7–8.

9. Williams, *Grace Hopper*, 8.

10. Edward Cowan, "Personality: A Can-Do Teacher of Finance; Roger Murray Is at Home in Classroom or in Board Room Columbia Professor to Have Charge of Fund's Investing," *New York Times*, May 2, 1965.

11. *New York Times*, June 18, 1932.

12. Cowan, "Personality."

13. Williams, *Grace Hopper*, 16.

14. Cowan, "Personality."

15. Cowan, "Personality."

16. See the interview with Peter Tanous in chapter 14.

17. Williams, *Grace Hopper*, 169.

18. Williams, *Grace Hopper*, 169.

19. Walter Isaacson, *Innovators* (New York: Simon & Schuster, 2015), 88.

20. Williams, *Grace Hopper*, 23–24.

21. Williams, *Grace Hopper*, 23–24.

22. Williams, *Grace Hopper*.

23. Williams, *Grace Hopper*, 114.

24. Isaacson, *Innovators*, 118.

25. White House, Office of the Press Secretary, "President Obama Names Recipients of the Presidential Medal of Freedom," November 16, 2016.

1. MURRAY'S FIRST CAREER: BANKERS TRUST (1932–1955)

1. Edward Cowan, "Personality: A Can-Do Teacher of Finance; Roger Murray Is at Home in Classroom or in Board Room Columbia Professor to Have Charge of Fund's Investing," *New York Times*, May 2, 1965.

2. Kathleen Broome Williams, *Grace Hopper: Admiral of the Cyber Sea* (Annapolis, MD: Naval Institute Press, 2013), 20.

3. Cowan, "Personality."

4. David J. Morrow, "Roger Murray 2d, 86, Economist Who Was an Advisor to Congress," *New York Times*, April 17, 1998.

2. MURRAY'S SECOND CAREER: INFLUENTIAL ECONOMIST (1950–1998)

1. Society of Actuaries, "Panel Discussion: Savings and the Economy," 19, part 2, no. 55 (1967): D322.

2. Society of Actuaries, "Panel Discussion," D323.

3. Society of Actuaries, "Panel Discussion," D323.

3. MURRAY'S THIRD CAREER: BELOVED AND RESPECTED BUSINESS SCHOOL PROFESSOR (1956–1978)

1. Edward Cowan, "Personality: A Can-Do Teacher of Finance; Roger Murray Is at Home in Classroom or in Board Room Columbia Professor to Have Charge of Fund's Investing," *New York Times*, May 2, 1965.

2. As a side note, Dean Brown oversaw the construction of Uris Hall, the business school's current home. The business school moved into its new buildings at Columbia's new campus on 130th Street in January 2022.

3. Because there were no computers, all trades were settled by the transfer of physical certificates. A runner was a messenger who literally transported certificates back and forth between firms.

4. *Financial Analysts Journal* (September–October 1984): 19.

5. Brian Thomas, ed., *Columbia Business School: A Century of Ideas* (New York: Columbia University Press, 2016), 32.

6. Kelly, *Financial History Review* (Summer 2020).

7. Dodd was dean of admissions when a young Warren Buffett applied to attend Columbia Business School in 1949.

8. *FAJ*, September–October 1984.

9. Douglas W. Cray, "Benjamin Graham, Securities Expert," *New York Times*, September 23, 1976.

10. Catherine Davidson, *Hermes, A Magazine for Alumni of Columbia Business School*, Fall 1987.

11. Cowan, "Personality."

12. Kathleen Broome Williams, *Grace Hopper: Admiral of the Cyber Sea* (Annapolis, MD: Naval Institute Press, 2013), 98.

13. Cowan, "Personality."

14. Williams, *Grace Hopper*, 98.

15. Davidson.

16. Thomas, *Columbia Business School*, 40.

17. Private letter dated April 27, 1992, from Gabelli to Murray.

18. Benjamin Graham and Doddsville, Fall 2011, 12.

19. Graham and Doddsville, 2011.

20. Graham and Doddsville, 2011.

21. Graham and Doddsville, 2011.

22. Private conversation, May 18, 2021.

23. "Paid Notice: Deaths Murray, Dr. Roger F. II," *New York Times*, April 16, 1998.

24. Kurt G. Hiebaum, "In Memoriam Roger F. Murray," Q-Group, Institute for Quantitative Research, internal publication, April 13, 1998.

25. Society of Actuaries, "Panel Discussion: Savings and the Economy," 19, part 2, no. 55 (1967).

4. MURRAY'S FOURTH CAREER: FUND MANAGER (1965–1970)

1. William C. Greenough, *It's My Retirement Money—Take Good Care of It: The TIAA CREF Story* (University Park, PA: Penn State University Press, 1991), 82.

2. Tanous interview, chap. 14 this volume.

3. Tanous interview.

4. Greenough, *It's My Retirement Money*, 84.

5. Penelope Orth, "Roger Murray: Portrait of the Professor as a Fund Manager," *Institutional Investor* 1968, 69.

6. Edward Cowan, "Personality: A Can-Do Teacher of Finance; Roger Murray Is at Home in Classroom or in Board Room Columbia Professor to Have Charge of Fund's Investing," *New York Times*, May 2, 1965.

7. Orth, "Roger Murray," 69.

8. Orth, "Roger Murray," 69.

9. Orth, "Roger Murray," 69.

10. Orth, "Roger Murray," 69.

11. Orth, "Roger Murray," 69.

12. Orth, "Roger Murray," 69.

13. Orth, "Roger Murray," 67.

14. Orth, "Roger Murray," 65.

5. MURRAY'S ROLE IN THE FORMATION OF THE PRIVATE PENSION INDUSTRY (1950–1980)

1. *Journal of Finance*, 7, no. 2 (May 1952): 252–59.

2. Congressman Eugene James Keogh, for which the Keogh Plan is named. Keogh represented Kings County, District 20 in Brooklyn, New York, from 1936 until he retired in 1967.

3. Tanous interview, chap. 14 this volume. All quotes in this chapter, unless otherwise indicated, are to this interview.

4. Leslie M. Rapp, "The Self-Employed Individuals Tax Retirement Act of 1962," *Tax Law Review* 18 (1963): 351–77.

5. Roger F. Murray, "Economic Aspects of Pensions: A Summary Report," NBER, 1968, https://www.nber.org/books-and-chapters/economic-aspects-pensions.

6. Murray, "Economic Aspects of Pensions."

7. *The Hunt Commission Report*, 1.

8. *The Hunt Commission Report*, 1.

9. *The Hunt Commission Report*.

10. Financial Analysts Research Foundation, 1993.

11. Kelly—MOAF.

12. *The Twenty-Fifth Anniversary of the Common Fund*, 10.

13. *The Twenty-Fifth Anniversary of the Common Fund*, 10.

14. *The Twenty-Fifth Anniversary of the Common Fund*, 10.

15. *The Twenty-Fifth Anniversary of the Common Fund*, 12.

16. *The Twenty-Fifth Anniversary of the Common Fund*, 13.

6. THE FIFTH EDITION OF *SECURITIES ANALYSIS* (1988)

1. Catherine Davidson, *Hermes, A Magazine for Alumni of Columbia Business School*, Fall 1987.

2. Davidson

3. Davidson.

4. Davidson.

5. Davidson.

6. Davidson.

7. Davidson.

8. Davidson.

9. Davidson.

10. Roger F. Murray, "Graham and Dodd: A Durable Discipline," *Financial Analyst Journal* (September–October 1984): 18–19, 22–23.

11. Davidson.

12. Davidson.

13. Murray, "Graham and Dodd."

14. Davidson.

15. Davidson.

16. Davidson.

7. REBIRTH OF VALUE INVESTING AT COLUMBIA BUSINESS SCHOOL (1993)

1. Roger F. Murray, "Graham and Dodd: A Durable Discipline," *Financial Analysts Journal* (September–October 1984): 18–19, 22–23.

2. Private conversation, May 18, 2021.

3. Patrick Verel, "Value Investing Giants Celebrated at Murray Lecture," *Fordham News*, May 6, 2013, https://news.fordham.edu/inside-fordham/value -investing-giants-celebrated-at-murray-lecture-2/.

4. Murray, "Graham and Dodd."

5. James Russell Kelly, "Roger F. Murray: The Bridge between Benjamin Graham and Modern Value Investing," *Financial History* 133 (Spring 2020): 25–27, 39.

6. Beverly Norman-Cooper, "Value Hunting: Columbia Students Bet on Ugly Ducklings," *Hermes* Fall 1994.

7. Brian Thomas, ed., *Columbia Business School: A Century of Ideas* (New York: Columbia University Press), 49.

8. Norman-Cooper, "Value Hunting."

9. Norman-Cooper, "Value Hunting."

10. Norman-Cooper, "Value Hunting."

11. Norman-Cooper, "Value Hunting."

12. Verel, "Value Investing Giants Celebrated at Murray Lecture."

13. Kathleen Broome Williams, *Grace Hopper: Admiral of the Cyber Sea* (Annapolis, MD: Naval Institute Press, 2013), 168.

14. Williams,*Grace Hopper*, 168.

15. "Paid Notice: Deaths Murray, Dr. Roger F. II," *New York Times*, April 16, 1998.

8. RECOGNITION AND AWARDS (1999 TO THE PRESENT)

1. Beverly Norman-Cooper, "Value Hunting: Columbia Students Bet on Ugly Ducklings," *Hermes* Fall 1994.

2. Norman-Cooper, "Value Hunting."

3. Q Group, Roger F. Murray Prize, https://www.q-group.org/roger-f-murray -prize/.

4. CFA Institute, CFA Institute Awards, https://www.cfainstitute.org/-/media /documents/corporate-record/award-recipients.ashx.

5. Brian Thomas, ed., *Columbia Business School: A Century of Ideas* (New York: Columbia University Press, 2016), 48.

6. Patrick Verel, "Value Investing Giants Celebrated at Murray Lecture," *Fordham News*, May 6, 2013, https://news.fordham.edu/inside-fordham/value -investing-giants-celebrated-at-murray-lecture-2/.

7. Verel, "Value Investing Giants Celebrated."

8. Verel, "Value Investing Giants Celebrated."

9. Verel, "Value Investing Giants Celebrated."

10. Verel, "Value Investing Giants Celebrated."

11. Verel, "Value Investing Giants Celebrated."

10. LECTURE 1—VALUE VERSUS PRICE (JANUARY 22, 1993)

1. Professor Eugene Fama shared the Nobel Memorial Prize in Economic Sciences jointly with Robert J. Shiller and Lars Peter Hansen in 2013. The Nobel Committee highlighted Fama's contribution to the market efficiency hypothesis when they awarded him the prize.

2. Murray was born in 1911. He joined Bankers Trust in 1932, during the early stages of the Great Depression.

3. The security market line is a concept of modern financial theory. The line displays the expected rate of return of a security as a function of systematic, nondiversifiable risk (volatility) and is the theoretical line on which all capital investments lie. Investors want higher expected returns for more risk; therefore the line slopes upward. On a graph, the line has risk (independent variable) on its horizontal axis and expected return (dependent variable) on the vertical axis.

4. Beta coefficient is a measure of how an individual asset moves (on average) when the overall stock market increases or decreases over time. The metric is used in modern finance to measure the volatility of a stock relative to the volatility of an index or the overall market.

5. Eugene F. Fama and Kenneth R. French, "Common Risk Factors in the Returns on Stocks and Bonds," *Journal of Financial Economics* 33 (1993): 3–56.

6. To Murray, a liquidity problem arises when an investor is forced to sell, thereby having no choice but to accept the market price available to complete the transaction independent of the company's intrinsic value.

7. Many investors focus on a company's free cash flow (FCF) as an alternative to reported GAAP earnings because of the potentially misleading nature of accounting conventions.

8. Murray always referred to this metric as "earning power." The current convention is to refer to the metric as "earnings power." You will see "earning power" in all the transcripts of the lectures because we did not want to alter Murray's content.

9. The Common Fund (Commonfund) is an asset management firm that was established to manage college and university endowments. The organization was founded in 1971 after a two-year study funded by a $2.8 million seed grant from the Ford Foundation. The fund launched with $72 million from sixty-three college and university endowments.

10. *Cap rate* is short for "capitalization rate." Although there is no common method for calculating a cap rate, it is often the ratio between the net operating income produced by an asset and the asset's current enterprise value. A cap rate is often used as a valuation method in real estate.

11. In 1993, the Institutional Brokers Estimate System (IBES) was the most widely used system for providing aggregating earnings per share estimates from brokerage firms for a company's financial performance.

12. An odd lot is an order amount for a security that is less than the normal unit (a round lot) of trading for an asset, which is typically 100 shares for stocks. Odd-lot trades were believed to represent retail investor activity rather than professional investor activity. Retail investors are thought to be less informed and potentially more emotional about their trading activity.

11. LECTURE 2—INGREDIENTS OF MARKETS
AND VALUE (JANUARY 29, 1993)

1. Professor Meyer Feldberg served as dean of Columbia Business School for fifteen years, from 1989 to 2004.

2. Value Line, Inc., is an independent investment research and financial publishing firm based in New York, founded in 1931 by Arnold Bernhard. Value Line is best known for publishing "The Value Line Investment Survey," a stock analysis newsletter tracking approximately 1,700 publicly traded stocks in over ninety-nine industries.

3. Murray is referring to the Dow Jones Average, which was at 40 points when he entered the business and was roughly 35,000 when we edited these transcripts.

4. FASB is an acronym for the Financial Accounting Standards Board. FASB's primary responsibility is managing the generally accepted accounting principles (GAAP) used by all publicly listed companies in the United States.

5. Lawrence Peter "Yogi" Berra was a professional baseball catcher who later managed the New York Yankees. Berra was known for his humorous-sounding statements, such as "It ain't over till it's over" and "When you come to a fork in the road, take it." Murray refers to the quote, "It's tough to make predictions, especially about the future." However, it is Mark Twain that said that quote, and Murray has erroneously attributed it to Berra in his reference.

12. LECTURE 3—EQUITY PRICING AND CAPITALIZATION
RATES (FEBRUARY 5, 1993)

1. Regina M. Pitaro currently is a managing director at GAMCO Investors, Inc., and the author of *Deals, Deals and More Deals.* Pitaro was a managing director at Gabelli Asset Management Company (GAMCO) at the time of the Murray lectures in 1993.

2. *Forbes* magazine publishes each year a list of the 400 richest people in America. Warren Buffett was number one on the list in 1993, beating out his close friend Bill Gates, CEO of Microsoft.

3. Mario Gabelli, Leon Cooperman, and Art Sandberg hosted a reception at the Lotos Club in New York City in 1988 to celebrate the publication of the fifth edition of *Security Analysis.*

4. Leon Cooperman is chair and CEO of Omega Advisors. Prior to founding Omega Advisors, Cooperman was chair and chief executive of Goldman Sachs Asset Management. He was a classmate of Mario Gabelli at Columbia Business School, and he is a former student of Murray.

5. CREF is an acronym for the College Retirement Equities Fund, which was established in 1952 as a division of the Teachers, Insurance and Annuity Association (TIAA).

6. Endpoint sensitivity refers to the potential misleading results caused by the dependency of the analysis on the starting and ending points.

7. An S-curve is a sigmoid function (logistic curve) that is used in economics to model the life cycle of new industries. The S-curve starts out slow, then accelerates, then decelerates, and finally levels off. Each stage of the industry's life cycle can be mapped to the S-curve to model growth for that stage.

8. The term *white goods* refers to large domestic appliances such as ovens, washing machines, clothes dryers, and dishwashers.

9. *Moody's Industrial Manual* was published for the first time in 1900, the founding year of Moody's. The manual provided information and statistics on stocks and bonds of financial institutions; government agencies; and manufacturing, mining, utilities, and food companies. Warren Buffett speaks fondly of flipping through *Moody's* to find compelling investment opportunities.

10. Franco Modigliani and Merton Miller, "The Cost of Capital, Corporation Finance and the Theory of Investment," *American Economic Review* 48, no. 3 (June 1958): 261–297.

11. Murray is referring to corporate bonds with a BA rating.

12. Statutory requirements for state-chartered trust and saving banks are part of the New York State banking law. As part of the regulation, the state Banking Commission issues a list of legally allowed investments for regulated institutions.

13. Wabash "five and a halves" refers to Wabash Railroad bonds issued with a coupon of 5.5 percent.

14. The Pennsylvania Railroad acquired Wabash Railroad in 1941.

15. Murray's reference to the "big book" is a reference to the rules and regulations for regulated trust institutions and saving banks.

13. LECTURE 4—CONVERGENCE OF PRICE AND VALUE (FEBRUARY 12, 1993)

1. Doug Jamieson is currently the president and COO at Gabelli Asset Management. He was executive vice president at the time of the Murray lectures in 1993.

2. Charles Bluhdorn, an Austrian-born American industrialist, was the long-standing CEO of Gulf and Western (G&W) Industries, a conglomerate he built over twenty-seven years. G&W owned blue-chip companies such as Paramount Pictures, Madison Square Garden, and Simon & Schuster.

3. Armand Hammer was an American business manager most closely associated with Occidental Petroleum, a company he ran from 1957 until his death in 1990.

4. Murray is referring to an investment approach where the investor buys several companies in the same industry rather than investing in a single company. With this approach, the investor is exposed to the investment opportunity of the industry without being overly exposed to the specific risk of each individual company because of the diversification from owning more than one company in the industry.

5. The agency problem arises when a principal (owner) of an asset hires an agent to manage the asset. Because the agent does not have the same incentives as the principal, the agent will act in her or his own self-interest, even if it is in conflict with the interest of the principal.

6. A poison pill is a shareholder rights plan used as a defensive tactic by a corporation's board of directors against a takeover. Typically, such a plan gives shareholders the right to buy more shares at a discount if one shareholder buys a certain percentage or more of the company's shares, thus effectively neutralizing any unwanted or hostile takeover. The term *poison pill* was coined by attorney Martin Lipton in 1982 in response to tender-based hostile takeovers.

14. FULL INTERVIEW WITH PETER TANOUS (1996)

1. Lawrence Chamberlain, *The Principles of Bond Investment* (New York: Henry Holt, 1927).

2. Gary P. Brinson, Randolph Hood, and Gilbert L. Beebower, "Determinants of Portfolio Performance," *Financial Analysts Journal* 42, no. 4 (1986): 39–44.

3. Representative Eugene James Keogh, for whom the Keogh plan is named. Keogh represented Kings County, District 20, in Brooklyn, New York, from 1936 until he retired from Congress in 1967.

4. Actually, it was the Keogh bill, which was later renamed ERISA when it was signed into law.